# THE JESUIT

# The
# Jesuit

A PLAY BY

**DONALD CAMPBELL**

PAUL HARRIS PUBLISHING

EDINBURGH

*First published*
*by* PAUL HARRIS PUBLISHING
*25 London Street, Edinburgh*
*1976*

*Cased* ISBN 0 904505 12 x
*Paper* ISBN 0 904505 13 8

*Published with the assistance of the Scottish Arts Council*

*Printed in Scotland*
*by* THE SHETLAND TIMES LTD
*Lerwick, Shetland*

# INTRODUCTION

We live in an age of disillusionment and desperation, an age which is characterised by a conspicuous absence of goodwill. All over the world, confrontations of one kind or another have reached the point of impasse, their participants having discarded peaceful means in favour of the apparently more persuasive arguments of the gun and the bomb. Social conflict — whether we call it 'urban terrorism' or 'freedom fighting' — has become part and parcel of a way of life for a great many people.

With so much blood being spilled to so little purpose, it all seems so hopeless. Yet the instigators of this violence are not evil. Mostly they are honourable men — intelligent, courageous, totally dedicated to the service of their chosen cause, men who are moved to oppose what they see as injustice, and who are prepared to carry that opposition to the point where they will sacrifice their very lives. No matter how honourable, however, they cannot expect to escape unscathed from the consequences of their desperate actions. Just as excessive violence has an ultimately brutalising effect, so too does extremism breed its own form of debilitating cancer — a certain attitude of mind which rejects all other attitudes and despises the people who hold them. Whenever a man resorts to desperate measures — in no matter how worthy a cause — he is in danger of succumbing to this life-denying (and, ultimately, self-destructive) attitude. The play you are about to read concerns the fate of one such man — he lived and died over three hundred and sixty years ago and his name was John Ogilvie.

John Ogilvie was no villain. On the contrary, the Roman Catholic Church, with every justification, have proclaimed him to be a saint. But did he really have to die that day in March, 1615? Was the Catholic faith really served by his death? Or did he offer up his life as a ritual sacrifice to a dogma which had become, for him, the only true reality? Did he cheapen his faith by putting its rituals before its teachings? Although

5

I have my own opinions on this matter, I realised from the outset that my opinions must inevitably be coloured by my own — Presbyterian — background and I have tried to be as objective as possible. I therefore leave my readers to answer the above questions for themselves.

*The Jesuit* was written in October, 1973. At the time, I had no idea of Ogilvie's impending sainthood and I doubt if it would have made much difference to the writing of the play if I had. I certainly made no amendments to the script because of the canonisation. The fact that the news broke at almost exactly the same time that *The Jesuit* opened was nothing less than pure coincidence. However gratifying this coincidence may have been for me personally, there is one aspect of it that ought to be mentioned in this introduction.

As is the case with most first plays, it was very difficult to persuade theatre managements to consider staging *The Jesuit*. Most agreed on its merits, but felt that it was too risky to produce on the grounds that it seemed to lack topicality and would not attract audiences. I myself had all but given up ever seeing the play on the stage. Then, one day in August, 1975, I bumped into Sandy Neilson and mentioned *The Jesuit* to him. From the moment he read the play, Sandy committed himself to it utterly, not only as Director but also taking over the very demanding part of Spottiswoode when Henry Stamper, due to personal circumstances, was forced to drop out of the production. Sandy's involvement, no less than my own, pre-dates the announcement of Ogilvie's canonisation and he deserves as much (if not more) credit as I do for the acclaim that *The Jesuit* has received.

Others, too, ought to be mentioned. Robin Lorimer, who gave me both his encouragement and the resources of his very considerable personal library when I was researching the play : David Campbell, who read the first draft, discussed the stage-craft with me and proclaimed his enthusiasm for the play long before it had reached the production stage : most of all, my wife Jean (to whom this volume is dedicated) who had the unenviable task of living with me throughout all the ups and downs that *The Jesuit* underwent. Lastly, there was George

6

Brown, who, with no thought or possibility of personal gain, worked and wrangled and worried his way through God only knows how many sleepless nights to get the production off the ground. To those — and many others too numerous to mention — I can only offer my undying gratitude.

DONALD CAMPBELL

Edinburgh, June 1976

# DEDICATION

*for Jean*

**THE JESUIT** *was first performed at The Traverse Theatre, Edinburgh, on May 4 1976, with the following cast:*

| | |
|---:|:---|
| **FATHER JOHN OGILVIE** | *MICHAEL BURRELL* |
| **ARCHBISHOP SPOTTISWOODE** | *HENRY STAMPER* |
| **LADY RACHEL SPOTTISWOODE** | *BETH ROBENS* |
| **ANDREW** | *ROY HANLON* |
| **WILL** | *JAMES YUILL* |
| **WAT** | *MARTIN BLACK* |
| **SANDY** | *KEN DRURY* |
| **DOCTOR** | *DAVID PEATE* |

*Directed by SANDY NEILSON*
*Presented by THE HERETICS*
*Stage Manager SUSAN BARRIE*
*Costumes designed by LINDSAY HARRIS*
*Lighting designed by GRAHAM DOTT*
*Production Manager DOLINA MACLENNAN*

"It has plesit God to cast in my hands a Jesuit, that callis himself Ogilvie . . . In his bulget we haif found his vestementis and other furniture for the masse with some bookis and reliques of S. Ignatius, S. Margaret, S. Katherin and other thair saints; also some writtis amongst qhiche the principal is a Catalogue of things left be Father Anderson, a Jesuit in Scotland qho semis to be furth of the countrey. Thairby your Majestie wil persaif the furniture of bookis and vestementis thai haif in store against the day they looke for, and sum of thair freindschip with qhom the samin is reservit." *Archbishop John Spottis-woode to James VI, October 1614.*

"If nothing could be found but that he was a Jesuit and had said Mass they should banish him the country and inhibit him to return without licence under pain of death. But if it should appear that he had been a practiser for the stirring up of subjects to rebellion or did maintain the Pope's transcendent power over kings and refused to take the Oath of Allegiance they should leave him to the course of law and justice." *King James's reply.*

"If the King will be to me as his predecessors were to mine I will obey and acknowledge him for my King but, if he do otherwise and play the runagate from God, as he and you all do, I will not acknowledge him more than this old hat." *Father John Ogilvie S.J., Speech at his trial, March 1615.*

---

*NOTES ON THE LANGUAGE*

OGILVIE speaks English with an officer-class accent.

SPOTTISWOODE speaks Scots, although I have used conventional English spelling for many of the words. This is to allow the actor freedom to modulate the degree of Scots in Spottiswoode's speech at different points in the play. For the sake of uniformity, I have used a similar orthography with Lady Spottiswoode.

THE SOLDIERS all speak an Edinburgh dialect of Scots.

12

# ACT ONE

## SCENE ONE

*Glasgow 1614. An ante-room in the provost's house at four o'clock on a bitterly cold October afternoon. The room is small, furnished only by a table, a chair and a short bench. On the table (which is on the left side of the room) is a decanter, two goblets and a jug of water. Opposite the table is a small fire-place in which a freshly-lit fire is blazing. The bench is between the fire and the table, lying along the wall beneath the window. The window is open and the howling of an angry mob can be heard outside.*

WILL *(off)* Come on, man! Get aff yer knees! Get a move on!

ANDREW *(off)* Dinna talk tae him, Wullie! For Christ's sake, dinnae jist talk tae him! If he winna move, gie him yer fuckin buits!

*ANDREW, OGILVIE and WILL enter from the right. The soldiers are contrasting types — ANDREW is a grizzled veteran, WILL a raw recruit. Both are plainly frightened but disguise their fear in different ways — WILL takes it out on OGILVIE and ANDREW takes it out on WILL. OGILVIE is a fair-complexioned man in his middle thirties. He has had a bad mauling from the mob — his face is a mass of scratches, his shirt is torn and open at the waist and a swordless scabbard is twisted round his back. He grips his cloak rather desperately in his right hand. He takes two steps into the room and falls, exhausted, flat on his face.*

*ANDREW goes to the window and pulls it shut, blocking off the noise of the mob which is, in any case, beginning to die away.*

13

WILL   Aw Jesus Christ! *(kicks* OGILVIE *in the kidneys and spits on him)* Ye papish bastard! Damn ye . . .

OGILVIE *groans and tries to rise, but cannot manage it.* WILL *kicks him again and* ANDREW, *hurrying across the room, shoulders* WILL *out of the way.*

ANDREW   Jesus Christ, laddie, ye've nae fuckin idea have ye? *Stepping across* OGILVIE'S *body, he turns him over and tries to lift him but cannot manage it. He grunts, straightens, and turns on* WILL *in a fury.*

ANDREW   That's right, Wullie, that's right! That's whit ye draw yer fuckin wages for — staunin there like a spare prick at a hooer's weddin! For Christ's sake, laddie, catch a grup at the ither end afore I catch a grup o you!

WILL *comes forward and together they lift* OGILVIE *on to the bench. He half-sits, half-lies there, shivering in a semi-conscious condition. They stand back and look at him for a moment, wiping their brows and spitting and generally assuming the attitude of men admiring a finished job.* ANDREW *turns and picks up* OGILVIE'S *cloak (which he dropped when he fell) and throws it over* OGILVIE'S *body.* ANDREW *then turns to the table and pours himself a stiff drink.*

WILL   Hi, hi, ye cannae dae that!

ANDREW   Cannae dae whut?

WILL   That's the Airchbishop's drink . . .

ANDREW   *(smouldering)* The Airchbishop — can get *stuffed!* *(takes off the drink)* Bluidy man, he can take a runnin fuck at hissel! And I'll tell him that when I see him anaa, you see if I dinna! Jesus Bluidy Christ, he's aff his fuckin heid! *(pours another drink and takes it immediately)* Twa men — twa men. A haulf-airsed wee laddie and a buggered auld man, no even twa real men tae tak a prisoner through thon rammy! Wullie, the man's a heid-case!

WILL   Aye, it was a haurd ane, richt enough! The mood thae

folk were in — tae tell ye the truth, Andro, I didnae think we were gaun tae make it! Naw! Christ, I dinnae mind tellin ye, Andrew, I was a wee bit feart gettin . . .

ANDREW  Aw, ye were, were ye? Well, thanks for tellin me pal! Thanks a lot! Because wance or twice oot there, I was gettin the distinct impression that you were aa set tae shoot the craw and leave me on my jaxy!

WILL  Aw, come off it, Andro! I wadnae dae that!

ANDREW  Too right ye wadnae! Too fuckin right ye wadnae! *(turns his attention to* OGILVIE*)* Look at him! *(laughs)* That's him! That's the lad! That's the lad that sterted aa the trouble! *(laughs again)* Christ, if this wasna sae serious, ye could piss yersel laughin at it! Whit that mob werenae gaun tae dae tae that puir bugger lyin there! And whit for? Whit for, eh?

WILL  *(with some embarrassment)* Hi, Andro, screw the nut eh?

ANDREW  Eh?

WILL  Ye ken fine!

ANDREW  Aw I dae, dae I? Well, I'm sorry, son, but I'm no shair that I dae. I'm no shair that I ken whit this boy's done — whit *ony* man could hae possibly done — tae turn the fowk o this toun intae a gang o fuckin animals. Because that's whit . . .

WILL  Aw come aff it, Andro, come aff it! Ye yen fine whit that oot there was aa aboot! That bugger there's a Pope's man!

ANDREW  A Pope's man? A Pope's man! The Pope, is it? Bugger the Pope! I didnae bring the Pope through thon rammy. I didnae risk my life for the Pope. And gin I did, son, and gin I did, they'd hae as little reason for it as they had wi this ane!

WILL  Aw, for Christ's sake, Andro! Whit's the matter we ye? Here, ye're no gonnae stert feelin sorry for him, are ye? He's a dangerous Jesuit priest! He's been sayin the Mass aa owre the place!

ANDREW  The Mass? Dae ye tell me that? *(whistles through his teeth)* Ha, that maun be a gey wanchancy thing tae dae, eh? Dangerous man, that. Aye, oh aye! Masses, eh? Jesus Christ. Dearie me. They'll shairly hing him for that.

WILL *(ignoring* ANDREW'S *sarcasm)* Serve him right anaa! B'Christ, hingin's owre guid for the like o that! See if it was me, I'd burn him. I'd pit the bastard on that fire here and nou! Papes, they're bastards! Bastards! I'd pit every fuckin pape in Scotland on that fire gin I had my wey; Every fuckin pape in Scotland . . .

WILL *advances towards* ANDREW *as he speaks, aimlessly wandering about the room.* ANDREW *seizes him by the lapels of the tunic and pulls him to his (*ANDREW'S*) face.*

ANDREW Ye little . . . *(He is so full of anger that he can say no more. He pushes* WILL *away from him with a gesture of contempt)* I'm sorry tae disappoint ye, son. He'll no hing. No for sayin masses.

WILL *(bewildered by* ANDREW'S *assault, has all but lost interest)* Naw? Will he no? *(suddenly realises the import of what* ANDREW *has said)* Whit for no?

ANDREW Because it's the law! This is his first offence — he'll maybe no even get the jile. Likely he'll get off wi a fine.

WILL A fine! Christ, dae you mean tae tell me . . .

ANDREW Aye. We brocht that man *(points to* OGILVIE *who has now recovered sufficiently to be able to sit up and take an interest in the conversation)* through aa that — and aa he'll get is a fine.

WILL A fine! It's no right, Andro, it's no right! *(pauses and thinks before he says any more)* Listen, Andro, if his kind got back, if the papes got the pooer . . .

ANDREW Wullie, Wullie, Wullie! *(gentler)* Wullie! Hou often dae I hae tae tell ye, son? Gin ye're gonnae be a sodger, gin ye're gonnae be ony kind o sodger — for Christ's sake, son, dinnae tak onythin tae dae wi politics!

WILL *Politics?* Whae's talkin aboot politics? This is religion!

ANDREW Politics, religion, whit's the fuckin difference in this

16

day and age? *(Suddenly weary, he passes his hand across his eyes and looks about him)* Whaur the hell has Spottiswoode got tae? Gode, I swear that man'll be the daith o me yet! He'll drive me tae the grave, b'Christ he will. See you that's talkin aboot Pope's men and religion? Well jist you keep an eye on the guid Airchbishop, that's aa! God, I whiles think he's hauf-roads tae bein a Pope's man himsel — and if we ever get anither Catholic King, I'll gie ye three guesses whae'll be the Airchbishop o Glesca! See if you want tae keep yer job . . .

WILL   Shote!

*Slow heavy footsteps are heard outside on the stair.* ANDREW *throws the dregs of his goblet on the floor and tries to dry the goblet on the tail of his tunic while* WILL *tries to straighten* OGILVIE *on the bench and bring him round by slapping his cheeks.* OGILVIE, *who is fully conscious by this time, pushes* WILL *away.* SPOTTISWOODE *enters. He is a biggish, heavy-set man in his middle age. He wears a long black cloak and a tight-fighting skull cap. Apart from the merest hint of a smile his face is quite expressionless. Both soldiers go to him and kiss his hand.* SPOTTISWOODE *never takes his eyes off* OGILVIE *from the moment he sees him.* OGILVIE *rises to his feet as soon as* SPOTTISWOODE *enters.*

SPOTTISWOODE *(A statement rather than a question)* This is the man.

ANDREW   Aye, m'lord. *(clears his throat)* We had a bit of a job bringing him owre, m'lord. The mob were — eh — unco coorse. We very near didnae manage . . .

SPOTTISWOODE *has been gazing thoughtfully at* OGILVIE *and listening to* ANDREW *with the slightest of attention. He now turns to* ANDREW *with a nod.*

SPOTTISWOODE   No doubt it went sair with ye. *(Looks at* ANDREW *expectantly)*

17

ANDREW *(sighs and takes a small pouch and papers from the inside of his tunic)* We fund this at his ludgins, m'lord.

SPOTTISWOODE *(taking the pouch and papers with a cursory glance)* Guid. *(Thoughtfully, with a dismissive shake of his head)* Attend me.

ANDREW *and* WILL *begin to leave. As they reach the door,* SPOTTISWOODE *suddenly, without turning, calls after* ANDREW.

SPOTTISWOODE  Andro!

ANDREW  M'lord?

SPOTTISWOODE  Gif ye think it is necessary to bawl at the top of your voice anent sic matters as the richts and wrangs of the orders I see fit to give ye — will ye please make an effort to moderate your language? It is — nocht seemly for the Airchbishop's man to be heard effing and blinding aa owre the Toun House of the Provost of Glasgow. *(He turns his head to look sternly over his shoulder at* ANDREW*)*

ANDREW *(without expression)*  M'lord.

SPOTTISWOODE *waves the soldiers away. When they have gone, he suddenly smiles warmly and shakes his head. He returns his attention to* OGILVIE, *going to the table, taking off his cloak and draping it over the chair. As he is taking off his cap, he speaks to* OGILVIE.

SPOTTISWOODE  Captain Roderick Watson, is it no?

OGILVIE *(somewhat shakily)* I think — perhaps it would be better to dispense with that name. It is a completely false one and to continue the pretence further would serve little purpose. My name is . . .

SPOTTISWOODE  Ogilvie. John Ogilvie. *(Drops his cap on the table)*

OGILVIE *(biting his lip)* That is perfectly correct. You have the advantage of me, sir.

SPOTTISWOODE *(amused)* Just so, Master Ogilvie. Just so. *(Rubbing his hands together)* Nou. Would ye take a dram? Ye look in sair need of it?

18

OGILVIE  That is very kind of you. I would be most grateful.

SPOTTISWOODE *picks up the goblet that Andrew has used, examines it for a moment, purses his lips and looks sceptically towards the door. He tosses the goblet in his hand, lays it aside and pours* OGILVIE'S *drink into a fresh goblet.*

SPOTTISWOODE  Water?
OGILVIE  Please.

SPOTTISWOODE *pours some water into the drink and hands it to* OGILVIE.

OGILVIE  Thank you.
SPOTTISWOODE  And you are of noble bluid, I understand?
OGILVIE  I am — and all my people before me.
SPOTTISWOODE *(conversationally)*  Sir Walter Ogilvie of Drum?
OGILVIE  My father.

SPOTTISWOODE *smiles and, sitting down, turns his attention to the papers. He begins to read, then looks up solicitously.*

SPOTTISWOODE  Sit ye doun, Master Ogilvie, sit ye doun. There is no need for you to stand.
OGILVIE  Thank you — but I prefer it.
SPOTTISWOODE *(with a slight shrug)*  As ye please.

SPOTTISWOODE *reads one paper, lays it aside with a sharp sniff of breath and frowns up at* OGILVIE. *He picks up the second paper and asks his next question casually as he spreads it out.*

SPOTTISWOODE  And you have been saying masses in the City of Glasgow?
OGILVIE *(mildly)*  If to do so is a crime, then it will be necessary to prove it — with witnesses.

SPOTTISWOODE *leans back in his chair and regards* OGILVIE *with a kind of stern speculation before he speaks.*

19

SPOTTISWOODE   To say the mass in His Majesty's Dominions
— ye maun be maist siccarly assured — is a crime. *(Leans
forward and re-commences his study of the paper.)* And I
have any amount of witnesses.

SPOTTISWOODE *spends little time with the second paper, laying
it carefully on top of the first. He picks up the pouch and
empties the contents on to the table. There are a number of
bones and a small hank of grey hair.*

SPOTTISWOODE   Oh aye. Relics. *(Picks up the hank of hair
rather gingerly between his thumb and forefinger and glances
enquiringly at* OGILVIE.*)*
OGILVIE *(crosses himself)*   A lock from the head of the blessed
St. Ignatius.
SPOTTISWOODE *(nods without comment, lays the hair down and
leans back in his chair with interlocking fingers)*   I am given
to understand that ye have been furth of Scotland this long
while — twenty-two year, to be exact, the maist of your
days?
OGILVIE   You appear to be remarkably well informed.
SPOTTISWOODE   Master Ogilvie, what garred ye return?
OGILVIE   My vocation.
SPOTTISWOODE   Which is?
OGILVIE   To save souls. *(Proudly.)* To unteach heresy.
SPOTTISWOODE   Indeed?   Sic a michty vocation would of
necessity — require a michty authority. But where is yours,
Master Ogilvie? Since ye did not get it from the King or
from any of his bishops . . .
OGILVIE   The King is a layman — as are all his so-called
bishops. None of them are competent to place authority,
spiritual authority that is, on any man.
SPOTTISWOODE *(slightly mocking)*   The *King* is a layman?
OGILVIE   He has not had his first tonsure — and he is certainly
not a priest!
SPOTTISWOODE   And you are?

20

OGILVIE *gives a little start, hesitates, then laughs.*

OGILVIE  Since you are so certain that I have been saying masses, you must be positive that I am a priest!

SPOTTISWOODE *(acknowledging the point with a faint smile and nod)* Aye. But let us return to my original question. From where do you derive your authority?

OGILVIE *pauses, looks seriously at* SPOTTISWOODE, *finishes his drink, and lays the goblet carefully on the table. Taking a deep breath, he delivers his next speech as if he were giving a lecture.*

OGILVIE  Christ's sheep were committed to the charge of Peter. Any man who would feed them must first seek his authority from the Apostolic See. Preserved there — through an unbroken line of succession — is the authority and power given in the first instance to the Prince of the Apostles. "Thou art Peter and upon this rock I will build my church; and the gates of hell shall not prevail against it!" *(Pauses and lets the passion of the quotation subside.)* Thus was Simon, son of John, made the strong rock of the Church that he might be Cephas and be called Peter. By the simple method of working back through all the Pontiffs, I can trace my authority to him — and through him to the Lord Jesus Christ.

*There is a short silence between them.*

SPOTTISWOODE *(with a sigh)* Aye. The Petrine Claim.
OGILVIE  The Truth.
SPOTTISWOODE *(sternly)* That, Master Ogilvie, is treason!
OGILVIE *(equally sternly)* That *Master Spottiswoode,* is faith!
SPOTTISWOODE *(snapping)* And ye would sign a declaration to sic effect?
OGILVIE *(hotly)* In my own blood if need be!
SPOTTISWOODE  I hardly think so. *Faither* Ogilvie. I hardly

think so. I hardly think that that will be necessary. Plain ink, no doubt will do just as well! *(Pushes his chair back savagely and walks a few steps away from* OGILVIE *before swinging round to address him again.)* It is the law of the land — the law of this realm — that the King — His Sovereign and Maist Gracious Majesty King James the Saxt — demands and is entitled to the allegiance and lealty of his subjects — of aa his subjects — in aa matters touching their lives. Aa matters — temporal *and* spiritual. That is the law. Did ye ken that?

OGILVIE  The law of the land is the law of man. The laws of God are not to be changed so readily.

SPOTTISWOODE  Maybe no. The fact remains that ye deny allegiance to the King in this matter and in aa religious matters?

OGILVIE  I do.

SPOTTISWOODE  And would render up sic allegiance to the Pope?

OGILVIE  I would.

SPOTTISWOODE  And if the Pope took it into his head to depose a king on the grounds of heresy, ye would uphold and support the Pope's richts in the matter?

OGILVIE  *(guardedly)*  I do not know whether the Holy Father has, or would claim such a right. It is true that many learned doctors of the Church have asserted that this is the case . . .

SPOTTISWOODE  Never mind the doctors of the Kirk, Faither. I'm speiring at you!

OGILVIE  It is not an article of faith. If and when it becomes so, I will die for it — and gladly. Until then, I do not need to pass an opinion to anyone — and certainly not to you. You have no right . . .

SPOTTISWOODE  Aye, Aye, I ken. I'm a layman. No had my first tonsure. I've no bloody rights ava! *(Pauses, looks seriously at* OGILVIE.*)* I must warn ye, Faither Ogilvie, that sooner or later, ye will be forced to answer that question. Your very life micht weill depend on the answer ye give. So. Aince mair. Gif the Pope took it into his head to depose a king on the grounds of heresy, would ye uphold and support the Pope's richts in the matter?

OGILVIE *(with some hesitation)* I assume you are asking me whether or not I would condone regicide. I fail to see why you cannot ask me the question straight out. I am opposed to regicide, Master Spottiswoode, I am opposed to murder — the murder of a king or the murder of a beggar. As a Christian and as a Catholic, that is the only answer I give you.

SPOTTISWOODE And gin I asked ye as a Jesuit, what answer would ye gie me then?

OGILVIE What do you mean by that, sir?

SPOTTISWOODE Let us get doun to specifics, Faither Ogilvie. There are others in your order who have less scruple when it comes to murder.

OGILVIE I haven't the faintest idea what you are talking about.

SPOTTISWOODE Oh, have you not? Perhaps I am being less than plain. Does not the name of Henry Garnett mean anything to you? Faither Henry Garnett and the Gunpowder Plot?

OGILVIE That is a monstrous slander! Father Garnett was a good and holy man!

SPOTTISWOODE *(snorting)* Holy man! Garnett was a traitor, a willing accomplice to the attempted murder of his king!

OGILVIE That is a lie! Father Garnett was executed by the English for refusing to betray a penitent — and he was not obliged to do that for anything in the world.

SPOTTISWOODE Ha! Was he no? Let me tell ye, Faither Ogilvie, that if any man was to confess sic a crime to me, I'd no lose much time in turning him in.

OGILVIE Nobody should confess to you.

SPOTTISWOODE Maybe no! But the fact remains that there was a Jesuit priest involved in the Gunpowder Plot. I ken that and so do you . . .

OGILVIE I know no such thing!

SPOTTISWOODE *(scornfully)* Ach, he was up to his oxters in it! What's more, barely a year of his Majesty's reign has gone by without some plot or intrigue or some scheme or other of a traitorous and seditious nature being uncovered. And on every single occasion there's been a Jesuit at the foot of it! And nou here you come owre from France with your English manners and your assumed name and *(snatches up the papers in his fist)* this neiveful of sedition in your kist. At this very minute . . .

OGILVIE    This is preposterous! What are you charging me with? If you're looking for traitors, why don't you try Robert Bruce? I'm told he lives near here and you have plenty of evidence . . .

SPOTTISWOODE    *(ignoring the question)*    At this very minute there are twenty-seven . . .

OGILVIE    Are you afraid to answer me then? Why don't you arrest a presbyterian traitor? Why don't you . . .

SPOTTISWOODE    *(shouting him down)*    Jesuit priests working against the well-being . . .

OGILVIE    What about the Seventeenth of September riots? Why don't you drag Robert Bruce in here?

SPOTTISWOODE    . . . and security of this nation.

OGILVIE    *(shouting almost into* SPOTTISWOODE'S *face)* What about Robert Bruce? What about Robert Bruce? Answer me, you imposter, answer me you *God-damned king-worshiping Heretic!*

SPOTTISWOODE *knocks* OGILVIE *down with a full-blooded punch to the jaw. He stands over him, panting with rage.*

SPOTTISWOODE    At this very minute, there are twenty-seven Jesuit priests working against the guid-keeping and security of this nation of Scotland — and I am Airchbishop of Glasgow and hae no need to answer to any one of them! *(Turns to the door.)* Andro! Andro!

ANDREW *and* WILL *enter at the double.*

SPOTTISWOODE    Take this man out of my sight!

24

ANDREW   Aye, aye, m'lord! Whaur tae?

SPOTTISWOODE *(angrily)* The Castle, ye fool! Where ither? Get me lowse of him!

OGILVIE *rises slowly to his feet as the soldiers advance. He stares at* SPOTTISWOODE *who has turned his back on him.*

OGILVIE   Who made you my executioner? *(Spits on the floor at* SPOTTISWOODE'S *feet)* And who made you Archbishop? Better butcher than bishop!

SPOTTISWOODE *(without turning)*   Get him away!

*The soldiers lead* OGILVIE *out.*

SPOTTISWOODE *goes to the table and pours himself a drink. He gathers the papers together carefully, re-dons his cap and picks up his cloak. Finishing his drink, he sighs and stares into space for a few moments.*

SPOTTISWOODE   Robert Bruce — oh damn Robert Bruce! *(Hurls the empty goblet into a corner of the room.)* God damn him!

SPOTTISWOODE *stamps out.*

### SCENE TWO

*The following January. A corridor in the Palace of the Archbishop of Glasgow.* ANDREW *is on his own, happed up for a journey and carrying a shield and spear. He looks distinctly cheesed off as* WILL, *similarly attired, enters briskly.*

WILL   Nae sign o them yet?

ANDREW   No chance!

WILL   Sandy's got aathing organised at the gate and Wattie and the ither lads are staunin by with the horses.

ANDREW *(nodding)*   Guid.

WILL Here, though. Gin we dinnae get a move on, we'll hae a job winnin awa. There's a fair crowd buildin up ootby.

ANDREW Ach, the Airchbishop's no bothert! No him! No wi *us* ridin aside him tae tak aa the stanes and glaur they'll be chuckin at *him*. Och! I'm fair wrocht tae daith wi aa this ditterin aboot!

WILL Whit are they jawin aboot, onywey? They've been in there for mair nor an 'oor!

ANDREW Christ knows! Ogilvie'll be argyin the toss again, I shouldnae wonder.

WILL *(laughing)* Weill, I hope the Airchbishop disnae lose the heid and thump him this time! Oh he's a funny ane that Ogilvie!

ANDREW Funny's no the ward. Bluidy bampot if ye ask me.

WILL Christ, no hauf! Tellt me aince — when I brocht him in his meat like — tellt me aince that he didnae mind the jile! Nae kiddin, Aye! Said he was servin his destiny, fulfillin his destiny — I cannae mind right what he said but it was somethin aboot his destiny. [And he's aye crackin bawrs and laughin, ken?] Aye that cheery. Damn shair I wadnae find muckle tae be cheery aboot gin I was in he's place! Christ, ye ken whit it's like in there, Andro?

ANDREW Aye. Oh aye.

WILL He's no been oot of that place for geynear three month. [It's cauld and it's damp and it's pitch-black and fair crawlin wi rats. And there's this muckle iron beam at the fit o the bed. Ogilvie's chyned til it by the ankles and it's a gey short chyn! He gets naethin but parritch tae eat and water tae drink.] If he's aff his heid bi nou, it's nae wonder!

ANDREW He was aff his fuckin heid afore he gaed in there if ye want my opinion.

WILL Aye. Maybe he was anaa! *(A thought strikes him.)* Here but! I didnae tell ye aboot this mornin. *(Laughs at the recollection.)* I gaed in there aboot — och, echt o'clock it wad be — brocht him in his parritch and some clean claes and that. *(Laughs again.)* He's lyin there, aa clairty and bleary-eyed among the rats and the shite *(laughs)* and his feet're stuck hauf-roads up tae the ceilin wi this bluidy chyn! I gets in there and I says tae him I says "Hello there, Faither! Hou're ye daein the day?" And ye ken whit? He's lyin there *(laughs and shakes his head)* and he says tae me, he says "Oh Will" he says — aa englified ken? — "Oh Will!" he says "It's past joking when the heid's aff!"

*They both laugh.*

ANDREW   Christ, that'll dae!

WILL   Past joking when the heid's aff! Oh Jesus — Andro, I geynear creased mysel! It was the way he said it, ken? Aa English and that *(mimics)* "Past joking when the heid's aff," Aw Christ!

ANDREW   *(serious again)* I wonder — maybe his heid'll really be aff efter they've done wi him in Embro.

WILL   Here, when we get hame — tae Embro like — what's the chances o a couple o days aff? I'd like tae get up the road — see my Maw.

ANDREW *grins broadly and chuckles to himself.*

WILL   What's the joke? Whit are ye laughin at?

ANDREW   Naethin. Naethin. It's jist — eh, want tae see yer Maw, eh?

WILL   Aye! I've no seen her for a while and — weill, I mean tae say, she's no gettin ony younger. Whit's the maitter wi that?

ANDREW   Naethin. Naethin at aa! *(Wipes the smile from his face.)* Aw, never mind, Wullie. Never mind, son. It's jist my sense o humour. I daursay we'll get some time away when we're in Embro — tae stert wi onywey. Later on, I'm no sae shair.

WILL   Later on? Are we gonnae be in Reekie for a while then?

ANDREW   A few weeks, I reckon. Depends.

WILL   Depends on whit?

ANDREW   Depends on hou muckle trouble they get frae Ogilvie.

27

Ach Ogilvie! Buggers like him gie me the boke, so they dae!

WILL The Papes?

ANDREW Naw! The nobility — nobility like thon! Rich men wi bees in their bonnets! Ach, they scunner me! I tell ye this, Wull — I've seen Ogilvie's like afore nou! He can caa hissel a Jesuit, a pape or whitever ye like — at the hinner end, he aye minds that he's Sir Wattie Ogilvie's son. And nae matter whit he's suffered here in Glesca, he kens up here *(taps his temple)* that the men that'll be sittin in judgment on him in Embro are his ain kind — gentlemen like himsel! sae he argies the toss, stands up tae the Airchbishop — aw he's the brave, brave boy richt enough! Crackin jokes and aa the rest o it! But aa the time, Wullie, he kens that he can say the ward and walk oot o here free as air! And he thinks that efter he's been in Embro and aa the talkin's done, that's jist exactly whit he's gonnae dae! But that's jist where he's mistaken, son. When we get tae Embro . . .

SPOTTISWOODE *(off)* Andro! Andro!

ANDREW At last! Christ, dinnae tell me . . . Come on, Wullie!

WILL *(taking* ANDREW'S *arm)* Andro, whit were ye gonnae say? Whit'll happen when we get tae Embro?

ANDREW *looks at* WILL *and grins.*

ANDREW Och, ye'll mebbe get tae see yer Maw! Come on, son. We're aff!

*Both exit.*


### SCENE THREE

*Edinburgh a few days later. Ogilvie's room in Spottiswoode's house in the Canongate. A barely furnished room containing no more that a bed, a table and two chairs.* OGILVIE *is seated at the table, writing. An empty chair is opposite the table.* SPOTTISWOODE *enters.* OGILVIE *glances up briefly but continues to write.*

SPOTTISWOODE  Guid afternoon Faither. And hou are ye the day?

OGILVIE *(continues writing, finishing with a flourish of his pen)* As well, my Lord Archbishop, as can be expected. Really Spottiswoode, these questions that you ask me are ridiculous!

SPOTTISWOODE *(raising one eyebrow)* It is your answers which interest me, Ogilvie — no your opinion of the questions. *(Indicates the paper on which* OGILVIE *had been writing.)* Ye have finished?

OGILVIE *rather sourly pushes the paper across the desk and walks away.* SPOTTISWOODE *seats himself on the empty chair and begins to read the paper.*

SPOTTISWOODE *(reading)* "Whether the Pope be judge and have power *in Spiritualibus* over His Majesty, and whether that power will reach over His Majesty even *in temporalibus* if it be *in ordine ad spiritualia* as Bellarmine affirmeth" Aye. Well, we aa ken the answer to that ane. Nane of us has the power to speir sic a thing of ye.

OGILVIE *(turning)* Nor I to answer such a question! Let us be quite plain about this — just what is it that you are asking me to pronounce on? This matter has been hotly contested by two of the most brilliant minds in Europe — namely King James and Cardinal Bellarmine. Father Francisco Suarez has also written on the subject and I, as a Jesuit and a good Catholic, naturally incline to the Jesuit and Catholic point of view — but, my good Spottiswoode, I am a very junior and unimportant Jesuit and it would be hardly fitting for me to enter publicly into such a controversy. Besides, what possible purpose could be served by any answer I might give? It would affect the issue neither way.

SPOTTISWOODE *(sighs and shakes his head incredulously)* Faither Ogilvie, whiles ye bumbaze me! Never mind. *Reads on* "Whether the Pope has the power to excommunicate kings (especially such as are not of his Church) as His Majesty?" Hmm. Faither Ogilvie, I fear that I am unable

**29**

to understand your answer. The Pope, ye say, can excommunicate His Majesty? I do not understand that.

OGILVIE  What is there to understand? Of course the Holy Father has the power!

SPOTTISWOODE  But — by your own argument — His Majesty is a heretic. And if His Majesty is a heretic, he cannot be a Catholic.

OGILVIE  *(with a long-suffering sigh)* A simple analogy. An outlaw is outside the law as far as the protection of the law is concerned — but he can be apprehended and tried and convicted by and according to the law. In just the same way, a heretic is outwith Mother Church as far as her blessings are concerned but is still subject to her justice — and to her punishment.

SPOTTISWOODE  I see. We are aa spiritual outlaws then?

OGILVIE  Yes.

SPOTTISWOODE  Even the youngest bairn baptised the day by a Calvinist minister?

OGILVIE  Yes. Yes. The Pope acquires his authority over man by baptism. Man enters Christ's flock through baptism and the Pope is the shepherd of that flock.

SPOTTISWOODE  *(sighs)* Man, d'ye ken what ye're saying? There's scarce a man in Scotland 'd have his bairn baptised under sic conditions!

OGILVIE  That is a matter of opinion. It may be true of those who despise Christ and serve the Devil — it is certainly not true of the faithful. And there are many more of these in Scotland than you, perhaps, imagine.

SPOTTISWOODE  *(sighs again, reads on)* "Whether the Pope has power to depose kings by him excommunicated? And in particular whether he have the power to depose the King, His Majesty." Aye. Aye. The auld sang. Nane of us has the authority.

OGILVIE  No.

SPOTTISWOODE  "Whether it be no murder to slay His Majesty, being so excommunicated and deposed by the Pope?" And here we are again! No spiritual jurisdiction! Can ye no, in aa conscience, give your opinion?

OGILVIE No.

SPOTTISWOODE Ye gave it to me! Ye told me that ye despised murder! Why could ye no have said the same to the Commission?

OGILVIE You have my answer there. You'll have to be satisfied with that.

SPOTTISWOODE *(reading on with a withering look in* OGILVIE'S *direction)* "Whether the Pope has power to assoyle subjects from the oath of their borne and natural allegiance to His Majesty?" *(Sighs deeply.)* With your customary arrogance, ye condem the Oath of Allegiance *(lays the paper aside).*

OGILVIE I most certainly do.

SPOTTISWOODE *bows his head wearily, rubbing the bridge of his nose between his thumb and forefinger. After a moment, he looks across at* OGILVIE.

SPOTTISWOODE Faither, d'ye ken wha framed these questions?

OGILVIE No.

SPOTTISWOODE Ye have no idea?

OGILVIE No. I assumed that it was a joint decision — yourself and some, perhaps all, of your colleagues on the Commission. Is it not so?

SPOTTISWOODE *shakes his head, taps the table, rises. He walks about a little, folds his hands purposefully behind his back.*

SPOTTISWOODE Faither Ogilvie, I'll leave ye without any doubts The answers ye have given to these questions will send you to the gallows. You are going to hang.

OGILVIE I am not afraid to die.

SPOTTISWOODE Aye, I thocht ye'd be pleased! *(Loses his temper momentarily, leans over the table towards* OGILVIE.*)* But I am nocht concerned with the smaa-boukit ambitions of your vanity! *(Turns away and faces about until his temper* *is under control.)* These questions are speired at you by no lesser person than His Gracious Majesty King James the Saxt of Scotland and First of England! *(Pauses to glower at* OGILVIE.*)* When ye were arrested in Glasgow — on that same night — I scrieved a letter to the King. I thocht — and still think — that ye were involved in a plot to murder His Majesty. Oh Faither Ogilvie, ye have been used in a maist merciful manner! *I* would hae given ye the boots — and micht yet! But His Majesty thocht otherwise. These questions were put to ye in order that ye micht have the chance to prove your lealty and allegiance to your King! Well, they have disproved it! They demonstrate quite clearly how small a value ye place upon your King and your country — the insolence and provocative nature of these answers will put a rope about your thrapple! Mind on that when ye mount the gallows!

OGILVIE  I do not know what you want of me. I have given the only answers I possibly could. I have replied with all the honesty and sincerity that I could muster.

SPOTTISWOODE  Certes, Man! It's not a question of honesty or sincerity but of tact! There's little wrong with the substance of your answer — it's the manner of the replies! Have ye read what ye hae scrieved? In every single instance — forby the ane anent the Pope's power of excommunication — ye deny the authority and jurisdiction of the King's Commission!

OGILVIE  Do you expect me to affirm it?

SPOTTISWOODE  Ye are no required to affirm or to deny! Aa ye had to say —aa ye *hae* to say is that ye do not ken! Ye'll get away with your answer anent excommunication — the King and the other Commissioners'll be as bumbazed as I was by it, but they'll no pay it muckle heed. As for the others, ye can just say what ye've just this minute said to me — ye are only a humble priest, no very important, and ye have no opinion in the matter.

OGILVIE  And such a reply would release me?

SPOTTISWOODE  No from the King's Justice. There's aye the

matter of the masses ye have said — ye maun be tried and punished for that. But ye'll no hang for saying masses.

OGILVIE  I see. *(Thinks about it for a moment.)* You are, of course, aware that I have yet to stand trial?

SPOTTISWOODE  *(irritably)* Ye'll stand trial when the nature of your crime can be determined. It is the purpose of the King's Commission to gather evidence for the trial. This *(indicates the deposition)* would make any trial for treason a formality!

OGILVIE  And if I answer as you advise?

SPOTTISWOODE  In any trial for treason, the process of law would be open to ye. In practice, I doubt very much whether sic a charge would be brocht.

OGILVIE  But I would be charged with saying masses?

SPOTTISWOODE  Of course. Charged, convicted and banished from His Majesty's dominions.

OGILVIE  You seem remarkably sure of the outcome!

SPOTTISWOODE  These are troubled times we live in, Faither Ogilvie.

OGILVIE  Indeed they are, Archbishop, indeed they are! *(Pauses thoughtfully.)* Why are you doing this, Spottiswoode?

SPOTTISWOODE  I beg your pardon?

OGILVIE  Why are you doing this? Why are you trying to persuade me to change my deposition? After all, you said just now that you believed me to be involved in a plot to murder the King. You are quite mistaken but I shan't argue about it — you are obviously persuaded otherwise. In your eyes, I am a potential assassin. Why should you seek to allow me to escape with my life?

SPOTTISWOODE  There are larger issues at stake.

OGILVIE  Larger than the King's safety?

SPOTTISWOODE  Larger than the life of one extremely ineffectual conspirator! Look, Ogilvie. If you are banished, I will be quit of ye — alive or dead, it's aa the same to me!

OGILVIE  *(with a deep breath)* Then I am afraid that it will have to be dead. For I cannot and will not change my deposition.

SPOTTISWOODE—Certes man, are ye wyce?

33

C

OGILVIE  Wise or foolish, I will not change my deposition.

SPOTTISWOODE  Damn you, John Ogilvie, for a bloody fanatic! What on God's earth d'ye hope to gain from this?

OGILVIE  Gain? I have no thought of gain. I am as in love with life as any man — but I will not change my deposition!

SPOTTISWOODE  But why, man, why? After aa I hae tellt ye?

OGILVIE  There are too many considerations. Far too many.

SPOTTISWOODE  Considerations? Certes man — there maun be plenty of considerations to gar a man die for his faith — there's nothing byordnar about that! But this is phraseology, a trick of speech, no mair nor that! With just a wheen changing of words, ye micht be as free as air! My God, man — ye cannae die for an attitude, a pose! Hou in the warld can sic a thing be justified?

OGILVIE  It can be justified because I justify it! That is enough.

SPOTTISWOODE  Pride!

OGILVIE  Not pride but dignity! The dignity of Mother Church. (Sighs.) You can neither understand nor sympathise. How can you when you do not know what dignity means? We speak in different tongues, Spottiswoode. You and I, we speak in different languages. When you accuse me of attitudes and poses, you do no more than judge me by your own standards. You call yourself Archbishop of Glasgow — what is that but a pose? What is that but a cynical attitude towards a noble and ancient office? You are no more Archbishop of Glasgow than I am — but it's little you care about that! You are quite happy to be an imposter as long as it serves your purpose. So I can expect nothing from you. (Suddenly angry.) But I know very well what you expect from me! You would have me go before this illegal commission and — what's the expression — play the daft laddie! That's it, isn't it? That's what you want. Then you would spank the daft laddie's bottom and kick him out of the country — kick *me* out of my own country — hoping, no doubt, that Catholicism would go with me! Oh My Lord Archbishop, how mistaken you are! I may not be more than a priest — and not a very significant one at that — but when I take my place before that court, I will

34

be the respresentative of the Church of the Risen Christ! And if my faith is to be defiled and humiliated in this land, this will not be the hand that does it! I will not change my deposition.

SPOTTISWOODE *(stonily)* Then ye maun take the consequences.

OGILVIE Do you think I'm not ready for that?

SPOTTISWOODE It will mean daith — and worse than daith!

OGILVIE *(scornfully)* Oh Spottiswoode, what a wonderful hangman you'd make! Do you think that I care in the least for your threats? [I haven't asked you for any favours and I never will.] I despise you, Spottiswoode. I despise you and your threats and your damned heretic malice! Do what you can and see if it makes any difference to me! I'll willingly suffer more in this cause than you and your henchmen can ever inflict!

SPOTTISWOODE Will ye suffer the boots?

OGILVIE Oh stop making those threats! Whatever you are going to do to me, do it! [You won't frighten me with threats! I'm not a hysterical woman, you know.] You don't frighten me! All you do is to give me fresh heart— your threats are like the cackling of so many geese! [Do what you have to do, Spottiswoode! Do not talk about it!] I am not afraid. When are you going to understand that? *I am not afraid.* All I ask is that, whatever you do, you do quickly.

SPOTTISWOODE The boots'll no be quick.

OGILVIE Damn your boots! I am not afraid of your boots!

SPOTTISWOODE Are ye no? *(Looks at* OGILVIE *thoughtfully for a moment, then turns to the door. He looks once at* OGILVIE'S *back before calling out.)* Wattie! Are ye there? Come in a minute. I want ye!

WAT *is a middle-aged man of medium height, rather squat in appearance and wearing a perpetually dour and surly expression.*

WAT M'lord?

SPOTTISWOODE *(to* OGILVIE*)* Wat is a great authority on the boots, Faither Ogilvie. (OGILVIE *glances over his shoulder at* WAT, *then looks away.*) I'll let him take a look at ye and then he'll maybe be guid enough to explain to ye just exactly what is entailed. Wat?

*Hands on hips,* WAT *walks slowly round* OGILVIE, *keeping a distance of approximately six feet between himself and the priest. He is carefully examining* OGILVIE'S *legs, behaving rather like a tradesman who has been asked to measure for a job of work and is making a preliminary inspection. Eventually he stops and addresses himself to* SPOTTISWOODE.

WAT I'll dae the richt ane first, m'lord. That's the usual. *(Squats beside* OGILVIE'S *right leg.* OGILVIE *eyes him apprehensively all the time.)* Generally get mair purchase on that leg. Mair muscle, ye see.

SPOTTISWOODE *(nodding)* Aye.

WAT Fower splints, m'lord. Ane here, *(indicating the inside of the leg)* ane here, *(indicating the outside of the leg)* ane here *(indicating the back of the leg)* and ane here *(indicating the front of the leg).* Fower tichteners. Ane at the ankle, ane on the shin — jist ablow the knee — ane on the thigh — jist abune the knee — and ane on the thigh again, jist ablow the hip. *(Stands up and stretches.)* There's been a wheen airgument aboot the best place tae drive in the wedge — Oh! *(Takes a wooden wedge from the inside of his tunic and holds it up for them both to see)* this is the wedge. As I say, there's been a bit o airgument aboot the best place to drive it in. Some say that ye're better wi the ootside o the leg *(laughs)* — I think that's daft. I mysel prefer to drive the wedge in on the inside. Ye get mair purchase, m'lord. D'ye understand? *(Demonstrates on his own leg.)* The wedge has got mair tae drive intae. *(Sniffs speculatively.)* Purchase is the secret in this game m'lord. Gin the wedge was big enough and I could get the purchase, I could drive it frae the tap o the hip-bane aa the way through tae the sowls o the feet!

OGILVIE *(hoarsely)* And how far will you drive it in my case?

36

WAT *(addressing* OGILVIE *directly for the first time)* Depends.
Depends mainly on the Airchbishop but it depends on yersel
anaa. I'll be hammerin awa wi the mallet richt up til the
minute I'm tellt tae stop.

SPOTTISWOODE *(all but crying out to* OGILVIE*)* Three blows of
the mallet will gar the marrow spurt from your banes!

WAT *(with some relish)* Jist sae, m'lord. Jist sae.

SPOTTISWOODE That will be enough for nou, Wat. Away ye go.

WAT *(taking his leave)* Thank ye, m'lord. *(Grinning wolfishly
at both of them.)* I'll be at yer service whenever ye need me.

*Exit* WAT.

SPOTTISWOODE Well. Nou ye ken what's in store for ye.

OGILVIE I certainly do.

SPOTTISWOODE And ye will not change your deposition?

OGILVIE No.

SPOTTISWOODE *(exasperated)* Ogilvie, ye are beyond me! I
swear your perversity leaves me speechless! Ye would thole
sic a torment as thon rather than make a reasonable
deposition . . .

OGILVIE *(incredulously)* Reason? What are you talking about?
The boots are hardly instruments of reason!

SPOTTISWOODE There would be no need for the boots — nor,
indeed any other method — if ye would but purge the
arrogance and pride from this deposition! Ogilvie, I beseech
ye — in the name of the Lord Jesus Christ I beseech ye —
do not make me do this thing to you. Change your deposition!
For the love of God, man, have some sense!

OGILVIE Sense? Who are you to talk of sense to me? We are
beyond that now. Good Lord, Spottiswoode, even if I had
been willing before to do as you ask, I cannot do so now.
Can't you see that? If I did, I would seem to have been
moved and led by feeling, like a beast — and not by reason,
like a man. [You cannot move me by reason and you will
not move me by feeling.] But try your boots, Spottiswoode!
Try them and see how far you get! Try your boots and I'll

37

show you that, in this cause, I care as much for your boots as you for your leggings! For I know myself born for greater things than to be overcome by *sense!* I put my trust in the Grace of God and you can do whatever you like! I will ask you for nothing — and I will neither alter nor add to anything I have said!

SPOTTISWOODE *(turning to leave)* Ye won't? Very well. Only mind on this — the pain ye suffer wilna be the pain of the martyr. Ye maun think what ye like — you are no martyr, John Ogilvie, and aa the suffering in the warld winna make ye ane!

*Exit* SPOTTISWOODE.

*Somewhat shakily,* OGILVIE *goes to the table and takes his seat. He draws a piece of paper towards him and begins to write. Before he has written two words, he breaks down and weeps uncontrollably. He beats his fist on the table repeatedly.*

OGILVIE I am not afraid! I am not afraid! I am not afraid!


## SCENE FOUR

*That same evening in the soldiers' quarters. The dining room or, more accurately, the room in which the soldiers eat. There is a longish table with benches on either side. On the wall, there is a rack where the soldiers hang their coats, swords, etc.* WILL *is at the table taking a meal. His sword and helmet are on the rack.* ANDREW *enters, whistling, a plate of food in one hand, a mug of beer in the other.*

ANDREW Ye got back then?
WILL Aye.

ANDREW *lays his food and drink on the table and talks to* WILL *as he unbuckles his sword and hangs it up, placing his helmet on top of it.*

38

ANDREW   Hou'd ye get on, well? *(Grins.)* See yer maw?

WILL   Aye.

ANDREW   *(coming forward and sitting down)*   Faimly aaricht?

WILL   No sae bad. Whit's the joke?

ANDREW   Joke?

WILL   Aye, ye're laughin aa owre yer ugly face. Whit's the big joke?

ANDREW   Nae joke, Wullie. Nae joke. Honest.

*WILL looks unsure, but does not pursue the matter. ANDREW grins and begins to eat. He eats quickly with plently of noise but no talk. When he is finished, he pushes back his plate, picks up his mug and grins at WILL.*

ANDREW   Come on well, let's hear it! Gie's aa yer news!

WILL   *(surlily)*   Naethin tae tell, Andro.

ANDREW   *(with look of disappointment)*   Aw here! Dinnae tell me! Dinnae tell me ye didnae get yer hole?

WILL   *(choking with outrage)*   Whit's that tae dae wi you?

ANDREW   But here I thocht we were gonnae be pals, you and me! *(Tongue in cheek.)* Comrades-in-arms, like?

WILL   There's some things ye keep tae yersel.

ANDREW   Aw haw! So ye did get yer hole?

WILL   Naw! I mean if I did — whether I did or didnae — I wadnae tell you!

ANDREW   *(shrugs)*   Suit yerself! *(Takes a slug of beer, grins wickedly.)* I did.

WILL   Eh?

ANDREW   I did.

WILL   You did what?

ANDREW   Got my hole.

WILL   Aw — ye did, did ye?

ANDREW   Oooh Aye! *(Stretches himself in reminiscence.)* Had tae pey for it like! Cannae expect onythin ither at my age. But, oh Jesus . . .

WILL   *(sighs, pulls a long face)*   Ye clairty auld tyke! And did ye no dae onythin else?

39

ANDREW Och, jist the usual! Gaed oot and got fou, got intae a fecht, got a hooer and got my hole. Whit else is there for an auld sodger? And forby — the toun's no the same.

WILL *(without much interest)* Naw?

ANDREW Naw! Ye'll hardly credit this, Wull, but there was a time I could walk through the Gressmerket and get stopped by every second bugger I met. They were aa my friens, I kent them aa. And nou? Nou they're aa deid — deid or no able tae get oot. I hardly ken a saul in Embro nou, son. See whit ye're comin tae? *(Takes another drink.)* Wha'd be a sodger, eh? Wha'd be a sodger?

WILL *(smiles)* Come aff it, Andro. Ye wadnae cheynge it!

ANDREW Huh? Dae I hae ony option? Still. Ye're richt, I suppose. It's been my life. And it's no sae bad in a job like this — nae action tae speak o, [forby the bit dunt wi the flet o the sword ye whiles dole oot jist tae keep yer haun in. Protectin His Lordship's presence frae the blandishments o a worshippin Glesca population!] Huh! Staunin gaird on heid cases like Ogilvie!

WILL Here aye! The Faither! Hou's he gettin on?

ANDREW Ogilvie? Ach, the sooner we're shot o him the better! I dinnae ken whit wey they dinnae jist hing the bugger and be done wi it!

WILL *(troubled)* Been actin up again, has he?

ANDREW Ach, ye've nae idea! Still, he'll soon be sortit!

WILL Hou's that?

ANDREW I reckon he's for the buits. The buits'll brak him.

WILL The buits? I've heard o them! Are they awfy . . .

ANDREW Aye they're a sair thing, laddie. An awfy sair thing!

WILL Ach, it's a shame! The Faither's no sic a bad sort o cheil, ye ken! It's an awfy pity! Ach, whit wey dae they hae tae torture him, onywey? They ken he's a priest, a Jesuit! That should be mair nor enough tae hing him! Whit wey dae they hae tae gi him the buits?

ANDREW Politics, Wullie. [I've tellt ye afore. Naethin tae dae wi us. Mair nor likely, Ogilvie kens somethin and Spottiswoode wants tae find oot.] Politics.

40

WILL   Well, I think it's a fuckin shame! [Gin his Lordship was gonnae gie the Faither the buits he should hae done it months ago, b'Christ! This is bluidy awful! ] *(Pauses obviously upset by the news.)* Will they get somebody in?

ANDREW   What for?

WILL   For the buits! Will they get somebody in tae gie them tae him?

ANDREW   Ye're jokin!

WILL   Well, wha gies him the buits then?

ANDREW   I'll gie ye three guesses!

WILL   *(jumping to his feet)*   Here, here, jist a minute! Screw the nut, eh? Screw the fuckin nut! I didnae sign on for that.

ANDREW   Ye're in the airmy nou, boy. And in the airmy — even this yucky wee airmy — ye dae whit ye're tellt! Which reminds me — ye better get awa up and relieve Wattie. The puir bugger'll be starvin bi nou!

*Rather reluctantly,* WILL *goes to the rack and takes down his sword and helmet.*

WILL   That's aaright, Andro, but I signed on for a sodger — no a bluidy torturer!

ANDREW   *(wearily)*   Forget it son! Forget it for nou! It wadnae be you that'd be rammin the wedge intil his leg in ony case . . .

WILL   Maybe no, but it's oot the bluidy box for aa that!

WILL *goes to the door, pauses, hitches up his sword.*

WILL   Ye'll be on the nicht watch?

ANDREW   *(absently)*   Aye.

WILL   See ye the morn then!

*Exit* WILL. ANDREW *sits staring into his drink. Eventually, he drains the mug and stands up.* SPOTTISWOODE *enters.*

ANDREW   *(turning)*   M'lord.

SPOTTISWOODE (raising his hand) It's aa richt, Andro, it's aa richt! Ye can stand easy! I'm sorry about this — hae ye finished your dinner?

ANDREW Aye, m'lord.

SPOTTISWOODE Guid. Well, get armed then and come on up the stairs. I want a word with ye. (As ANDREW gets ready.) Ogilvie, Andrew. It's about Ogilvie. What d'ye think?

ANDREW (belting on his sword) He'll brak gif ye gie him the buits, m'lord. Shair as daith!

SPOTTISWOODE Mm. Ye dinnae care for the boots, do ye Andro?

ANDREW I'm a sodger, sir. It's aa in the days wark.

SPOTTISWOODE Aye, aye, aye. But ye dinnae care for them, do ye. Yersel, I mean! It's no a job ye like?

ANDREW Wattie's yer man for the buits, m'lord. No me. (Hesitates.) As I say, I'm a sodger — I'm trained tae fecht, no torture. Naw sir, I dinnae care for the buits.

SPOTTISWOODE I'll be frank with ye, Andro. Neither do I. And in this case — in this case I question their effectiveness. I'm thinking that it micht be better to consider something else.

ANDREW (all ready) Whatever ye say, m'lord.

SPOTTISWOODE Come away up the stair. We'll hae a blether aboot it.

*Exit* SPOTTISWOODE, *followed by* ANDREW.


## SCENE FIVE

OGILVIE'S *room, nine days later. The bed has been removed and* OGILVIE *is seated at the table. He is a terrible sight. His shirt is torn to shreds, his hair is in disarray, there are enormous black rings about his eyes and scratch-marks and streaks of blood all over his hands and arms. He has been denied sleep for the past eight days.*

*It is four o'clock in the morning.* ANDREW, *on the night*

*watch, is seated on the edge of the table. He has shed his sword, helmet and tunic and has no other weapon except for a dagger which he keeps in a leather sheath strapped to his bare arm.* OGILVIE'S *head falls on his chest and his eyes close.* ANDREW *slaps him hard across the face several times.*

ANDREW  Come on, Faither, come on! Ye ken ye cannae get tae sleep! *(*ANDREW'S *slapping has had no effect so he draws the dagger and jabs at* OGILVIE'S *shoulder several times.)* Wake up, man, wake up, wake up!

OGILVIE *staggers back out of his chair like a startled beast. He stumbles once or twice but eventually manages to stand up fairly steadily, albeit in a stooped position.*

OGILVIE *(peers in* ANDREW'S *direction, shading his eyes with his hand)* Who — who is it this time? Andrew? Is it you, Andrew? You'd never believe . . . Is it you, Andrew? Yes. Yes, it *is!* It *is* you, Andrew. I know it is. [You're the one.] You're the one who never says anything. You never say anything. Well, very little anyway. So it must be you, Andrew. It must be . . .

ANDREW  Aye, Faither, it's mysel.

OGILVIE  Oh. Oh. I knew it. I knew all the time that it was you. I knew it but I hoped — oh, never mind! I hoped — I hoped it might be one of the others. Because you're the worst, Andrew, did you know that? [The worst, the very worst of the lot.] The very worst *(laughs)* of a bad, bad lot! *(Laughs louder.)* The Praetorian Guard of His Heretical Holiness! *(Bitterly.)* Bunch of workshy know-nothings and broken-down has-beens! Sandy — God, Sandy's bad enough! He talks and talks and talks and talks. He hardly stops for breath. His tongue chisels away all the way into the farthest extremities of my brain! Oh, I know all about you, Andrew — what a great warrior you were, all the battles that you fought! Sandy makes it sound like some great legend *(laughs)* — a great legend that goes on and on and on and on! *(Shakes his head.)*

43

[Sandy — poor Sandy — Sandy is a bore.] But he's not the worst — no, no, not by a long chalk he's not the worst. Neither is Will — oh my God, Will, Will, what am I saying? Will's the best! The only one of the whole damned lot of you with a morsel of charity in him. He's a good boy, Wullie — a very good boy. Now don't mistake me! Don't misunderstand! He does his job, he keeps me awake — nothing else you hear? *(Softer.)* But he's kind. He's considerate. He talks to me — he talks to me without shouting, without argument, without — without — without . . . oh dammit, what's the word, what's the word! What I mean to say is that, when he talks to me he listens to what I say, there are no barriers between us, no implacable stone walls! I have not talked to another living being, the way that I sometimes talk with Will, for many a long, long day. And perhaps I never will again. And if he could just — if I could get him to — Oh, no, no, no, it's useless, useless! He will not listen. He's a heretic, another damned heretic just as you . . . just as you *(gives* ANDREW *a shifty suspicious look)* all are! *(Whispers.)* Andrew? Andrew? Is that right? Are you a heretic?

ANDREW  Eh?

OGILVIE  A heretic. I asked you if you were a heretic. Are you a heretic?

ANDREW  If ye say so, Faither.

OGILVIE  No! *Not* if I say so! *I* am not *you!* It's not for me to tell you whether or not you are a heretic. It's not for me to say! It's for you. You. It's your own decision! The facts are before you, you can make up your own mind. You don't *have* to be a heretic, you know. You don't have to be! *(Suddenly weary, he passes his hand across his eyes.)* I was a heretic once, did you know that?

ANDREW  *(more to himself than to* OGILVIE*)* Wadnae surprise me, Faither.

OGILVIE  Eh? What was that? What did you say? It wouldn't surprise you. It wouldn't surprise you, eh? Why not? Why not, pray? Do I look like a heretic! Do I sound like a heretic!

Do I behave like a heretic? What am I doing here if it would not surprise you?

ANDREW *(uneasily, not really wanting to talk)* Jist passin a remark, Faither. Didnae mean ocht by it.

OGILVIE No? No? It occurs to me Andrew, that you do not care for heretics. Is that right? *(ANDREW says nothing.)* [Now Andrew. I asked you a question. I want an answer. I get the distinct impression that you do not greatly care for heretics. Andrew, am I right.] *(Again ANDREW says nothing.)* Andrew, I am talking to you! I am asking you a question and I want an answer right now. Do you or do you not care overmuch for heretics? *(Still ANDREW says nothing. OGILVIE bunches up his fist and shakes it at him.)* You! You! You! Oh you! I might as well try to communicate with a rock as bother with you! [You are always this way. You hardly say a word.] Sandy speaks too much and you speak too little and Wat *(recoils as if in pain).* Wat! Oooh that twisted pig, Wat! *(Holds out his hands to ANDREW.)* Have you seen this, Andrew? Have you seen Wat's latest? Clever wee Wattie's latest trick to torment Father Ogilvie? He took ten nails, Andrew, ten nails and drove them — one at a time, with his mallet — right under my fingernails! Oh, the cunning little bastard, why did he have to do that! [His ingenuity, his bestial ingenuity knows no bounds! ] *(Pauses to recover his somewhat fragile composure.)* And yet and yet, I'll tell you something — I prefer, I *much* prefer Wat to you. Yes. Yes. His torture, his physical torture, is far more bearable that the torment that your silence inflicts on me! *(Pauses to gather his thoughts and put them into words.)* Wat enjoys himself you know — he *enjoys* himself. [You'd never guess it from his expression — that dour, heretical, swinish little face — but he *does* enjoy himself. Everything he does— every new source of pain that he invents comes from up here. *(Taps his head.)* Nobody tells him, Nobody gives him orders — how he must think and rack his brain for originality! He brings his tortures to me with all the enthusiasm and delight of a devoted father with gifts for his new baby! Mind you, there's nothing personal in it! It

45

has nothing to do with *me!* But I am a Catholic, you see — and Wat is strong, strong against the papes! Oh aye! So he doesn't worry about me at all — and he enjoys himself. But Andrew — it works both ways. D'you understand what I mean? D'you understand? D'you understand what I'm trying to say? Wattie doesn't think of me as a human being at all — that's why he can approach his work with so much equanimity. But, you see, it works both ways — I don't think of him as human either! No!] And when he was hammering those nails into my hands, there was a part of me — not all of me, I admit, just a part, a small part — that was enjoying it every bit as much as he was! Can you understand that? Eh? *(ANDREW looks sceptical but says nothing. OGILVIE laughs.)* You don't believe me, do you? You don't believe that anyone could enjoy it! *(Thrusts his hands in front of ANDREW'S eyes so viciously that ANDREW recoils, reaching for his dagger.)* But I did, I tell you — I did. You see, [Andrew, when Wat was tapping in the nails — the nails into my fingers] — there were no complications, no extraneous considerations. There was a confrontation going on, a divine confrontation, that had nothing to do with Wat or myself, with the logic or wisdom of my beliefs or the logic or wisdom of his, with his cruelty or my pain. No, no, it was more than that, much more. We were only the instruments, we were only the instruments, the weapons of a conflict that was ultimately between the Almighty on my side and the Devil on his. Now do you understand why I hate you more than the others? Now do you understand why I asked you that question? Now do you understand why I *must* know what you feel about heretics? *(He has wound himself up almost to breaking point and now begins to weep).* Why don't you answer me? Why don't you say something? Why do you just stand there and smirk?

ANDREW Naethin to say, Faither!

OGILVIE That's what you always say! *(Mimics)* "naethin to say, Faither". Don't try to fool me, Andrew. Don't try to pretend to me that you are a man of few words — because

46

I know different! *(Turns wearily away, worn out by his fury but turns back almost immediately in a more composed, if intense, vein.)* [Andrew. I am not a fool. I'm not a child. Eh? I know, you know. I know why you won't talk to me.] I know. You will not talk to me, you refuse to talk to me, you are afraid to talk to me because you *(points)* are a Catholic!

ANDREW *gives a scornful, embarrassed laugh but says nothing.*

OGILVIE How long have I been without sleep, Andrew. How long? Must be — a week? Must be. Eh? Is it a week? It must be that at least! Even so. Even so, Andrew, after all this time, after all this time without my natural rest — even so, there are periods, there are short spells when I have complete, absolutely complete lucidity. There are periods when I am as awake and as aware as ever I was. And believe me, Andrew, I am fully awake now! *(Goes quickly to* ANDREW *and takes him by the shoulders.)* Andrew, I am going to ask you a question. I am going to put a question to you. And if you refuse to answer — or if you should answer falsely — Andrew, oh Andrew, Andrew you will surely be damned! *(Takes a deep breath.)* Now. Tell me. Are you or are you not a Catholic?

ANDREW *(hesitates, looks* OGILVIE *in the eye, turns away)* That was a while syne. A lang while syne.

OGILVIE *(exulting)* You are! You are! I knew it! I knew it! You are a Catholic. Heaven be praised!

ANDREW *(angry and embarrassed and evasive all at the same time)* My faither was! My mither was!

OGILVIE *(without noticing the evasion)* Your mother — your mother was a Catholic? Is that right? Is that right now, Andrew? *(Turns away as if in a dream.)* So was mine, Andrew. So was mine. Oh Andrew, it is the Catholic women who are the backbone of our faith — the Catholic women. There are many — I myself have known many, a great many men who were holy, truly holy. But I never met any man who was as holy as my mother. *(Closes his eyes as if in prayer.)*

Oh you are a woman of great faith. What you have desired will be accomplished for you. *(Turns again to* ANDREW.*)* Tell me, Andrew. Where do you worship?

ANDREW *(amused)* Worship, Faither?

OGILVIE Worship. Yes. Where do you worship? Where do you receive the Mass.

ANDREW *(shaking his head)* I never worship, Faither.

OGILVIE *(shocked)* Never.

ANDREW Naw!

OGILVIE Then how . . . how do you serve your faith?

ANDREW Faither *(with some hesitation)* I hae nae faith.

OGILVIE No faith? No faith? This — what d'you mean, you've lost your faith? Is that it? Have you become a heretic? *(*ANDREW *turns away, says nothing.)* Answer me, Andrew. Answer me. You're not going to turn dumb again, are you? Just when you've started to talk? Don't you understand, Andrew? Don't you understand that I cannot bear those silences? I cannot bear your terrible silences!

ANDREW *(savagely)* Faither, I hae nae faith. Leave it at that!

OGILVIE But Andrew — a man cannot live without faith!

ANDREW *(turns savagely once more, suddenly smiles gently)* Faither, I am forty-twa year auld.

OGILVIE Oh Andrew. Oh Andrew, Andrew, Andrew. Oh — Oh Scotland. What kind of country have you become? [What depths of barbarism have you reached?] When a man can stand before his priest without shame and tell him that he has lost his faith! *(Turns to* ANDREW *again.)* So. You are beyond even the evil sin of heresy. You are a pagan. You have lost your faith. *(Suddenly savage.)* Well, I have not lost mine! That is why I am here. That is why I am enduring this — this torment! That is why I will endure all this and more! Spottiswoode — did you know that Spottiswoode threatened me with the boots. Yes. The boots. *(Smiles and shakes his head.)* I think he broke poor Wattie's heart when he decided not to use them. And he told me — Spottiswoode did — he told me, he said to me that I was lucky. Lucky! *(Mimics)* "Ye hae been used in a maist merciful manner, Faither Ogilvie".

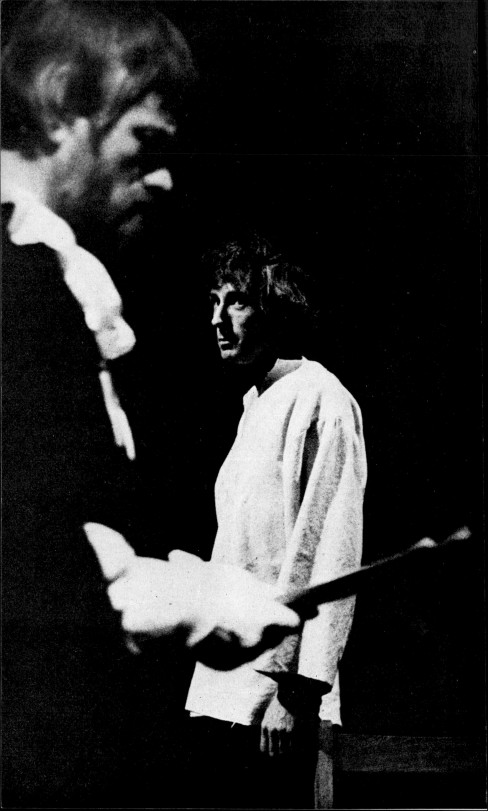

*(Laughs bitterly.)* You're all fools, do you know that? *(Slaps his leg.)* What's this. Eh? It's a leg. That's all. A leg. What good is a leg to a priest? To carry him into chapel, that's all. To carry him into chapel. *I can be carried into chapel!* Don't you understand? Take my leg, take both my legs! Take my arms! I do not need them, they are of no use to me! But you, you . . .

*Suddenly he screams and staggers about with his head in his hands.* ANDREW *stands by, aghast and helpless, looking towards the door every now and again as if unsure about going for help.* OGILVIE *turns on* ANDREW *forcing him up against the wall and ranting at him in a voice that seems stretched to breaking point:*

OGILVIE You, you you, what are you doing? What are you doing to me? What are you doing? You are driving a wedge into my mind! You are crushing my brains and my reason is running from my skull in rivers of grey! *(Pushes himself away from* ANDREW *who now seems considerably alarmed.)* You are driving me mad! You take my mind, you take my body, you take my reason, you take my comfort. Very well, then! Take it — take it all! I have no use for it, for any of it! I tell you only this *(gathers himself together in one last defiant bellow). You shall not have my faith!*

OGILVIE *collapses.* ANDREW *rushes to him and tries to bring him round, without success. He goes to the door and bangs on it repeatedly.*

ANDREW Sandy! Sandy! Whaur are ye, ye donnert bugger! Wake up, for Christ's sake! I want ye!
SANDY *(off)* Is that yersel, Andro?
ANDREW Whae the bluidy hell d'ye think? Come in here, for Christ's sake! I'm needin ye!

*The door opens and* SANDY *enters. He is a wiry little man, extremely talkative and of roughly the same age as* ANDREW.

49

SANDY  Is it the Faither? I heard aa the rammy. Away again, is he?

ANDREW  Aye. Come on, gie's a haun wi him.

ANDREW *bends over* OGILVIE'S *body, taking him by the armpits.* SANDY *follows, dithering and talking all the time.*

SANDY  My my my my, Andro, I'll tell ye straucht. I cannae be daein with this wey o warkin. I tellt the Bishop, I says tae him, I says . . .

ANDREW  Shut yer bluidy face and get on wi it!

SANDY  *(unperturbed)* . . . this offends my sense o professional decorum . . .

ANDREW  *(struggling with* OGILVIE*)* Jesus Christ, Sandy! Get him up! *(Together they manage to get* OGILVIE *to his feet.)* Right. Twice roun syne let him faa. Come on.

*They half-walk, half-drag* OGILVIE *twice round the room.* SANDY *keeps on talking.*

SANDY  They'd hae been far, far better wi the buits — far far better. I've said frae the start that this was a daft-like wey o warkin — wastin aa this time and no even a cheep of whatever it is the Airchbishop wants. Ye can say whit ye like, Andro. Ye can say whit ye like. It's jist no right that professional sodgers like you and me should be asked tae tak on duty like this. This is Wattie's game, this. The torture tredd. It micht be aaricht for Wattie — aye, it micht be aa very weill for Wattie! No for me. I ken wappins, I tellt the Bishop, I ken wappins, been a sodger aa my days, that's *my* tredd. I says tae Spottiswoode I says . . .

ANDREW  *(with long-suffering patience)* Are you fuckin finished?

*They have once more reached the centre of the room.*

SANDY  *(slightly cowed)* Weill, ye ken whit I mean.

ANDREW  Dae I? Jesus Christ, I sometimes wonder if ye ken yersel! Have ye got him?

**50**

SANDY *(taking a firmer grip on* OGILVIE'S *arm)*  Aye.
ANDREW  Are ye ready?
SANDY  Aye.
ANDREW  Right. Wan. Twa. Three.

*They stand back and allow* OGILVIE *to keel forward on his face.* OGILVIE *rises to his hands and knees and shakes his head.*

OGILVIE *(rising)*  My God. Oh My God. *(Shouting.)* My God!
I have kept my promise! I have made you known to the men
you gave me! [I have given them your word and they have
received it! My God, My God, I pray for them, these men.
I pray for them and them alone because these are the men
you gave me. Let them be with me, Oh Lord! Let them be
with me in my hour of glory. Let them be with me in the glory
you will give me!] Let them be with me that they might see,
that they might know that the glory that is mine is the glory
of Almighty God! Father, the world does not know you as
I know you . . . the world does not know . . . Father . . .
the world . . .

*He is reeling and tottering and obviously about to fall over
again.*

ANDREW  Watch him!

ANDREW *and* SANDY *manage to catch* OGILVIE *safely but his
falling weight makes both of them stagger back. They stand,
holding* OGILVIE, *and panting for breath.*

SANDY  Jesus Christ! Andro, he's weill awa nou. Did ye hear
whit he was sayin? He's haverin nou — we'll no get onything
oot o him gin we keep this up! He'll no last the nicht. Aw
Andro, when I think o aa that you and me hae seen
through thegither — I never thocht I'd see the day that . . .
ANDREW  Shut up, Sandy! Shut up! Gie yer fuckin erse a
chance, will ye? Christ, ye never stop!

51

SANDY *(hurt by* ANDREW'S *rebuke)* I'm sorry, Andro. I didnae mean tae . . . Will we tak anither turn?

ANDREW Naw, naw, it'll dae nae guid. We'd jist tire ane anither oot. We'd better gie the drap anither try tho. Are ye ready?

SANDY Aye.

ANDREW Richt. Wan. Twa. Three.

OGILVIE *keels forward again.* ANDREW *and* SANDY *go to him.* ANDREW *kneels down and listens to his heart.*

OGILVIE You're damned, Andrew! You are going down to the burning fires of hell! You have thrown away your faith and you cannot be saved or released from your damnation! God is not mocked, Andrew, God will not be mocked. I know where you are, I know where you live. I know the spirit that burns within you, the flame, the dying flame, the dying flame which yet might live! [Wake up, Andrew, before it's too late and the fire consumes you. Wake up, wake up, wake up! Feed that flame that it might not die! ] There are few here in Scotland who have kept their clothes clean — but wake up, only wake up and I tell you that you will walk with me dressed in the purest of white raiment. You will walk with me dressed in the raiment of the blessed of Christ. Oh, I know you do not love me as you must have done once — I know you do not love me now as you did then. Only turn from your sins and do as you did then — turn from your sins, I beseech you, turn from your sins! For if you do not turn from your sins I will come and I will find you and I will leap upon you like a thief in the night! Listen to me, Andrew! Listen to me if you have ears! Listen to me if you have ears! Listen to me if you have ears!

OGILVIE *collapses once again and this time,* SANDY *and* ANDREW *are so horror-struck by him that they do not even try to catch him. He lies on the floor gabbling for a moment before passing out again.*

SANDY *(breathlessly)* He's gane badgy!

52

ANDREW *(glancing dazedly at* SANDY*)* Guid God! Guid God!

SPOTTISWOODE *enters briskly, followed by a* DOCTOR, *a severe-looking young man.*

SPOTTISWOODE What's happening here? What's the trouble? Andrew?

THE DOCTOR *goes to* OGILVIE *and starts examining him.* ANDREW *takes a step back and looks at* SPOTTISWOODE, *shaking his head.*

SANDY Gin ye want my opinion, M'lord, I'd say that he's gey near it. I mean to say, sir, echt days and nine nichts, I mean tae say . . .

SPOTTISWOODE *(completely ignoring him)* Andro. What d'ye think?

ANDREW *(hesitates before he answers)* I dinnae ken, m'lord. Shair as daith, I dinnae ken. I thocht that . . . weill, I didnae think he had it in him, I didnae think he had the smeddum tae see it through this far. And nou — nou I hae the idea, I'm jist as shair that he'll see it through till daith. Daith and worse nor daith. I think he's past tholin ony mair o it.

DOCTOR M'lord, gin this man is no let to sleep within the hour, he'll no survive.

SPOTTISWOODE Ye're siccar o that?

DOCTOR Aye, m'lord.

SPOTTISWOODE *paces the floor, hands behind back, deep in thought.*

SPOTTISWOODE Very well. Andro. Sandy. Bring him a bed.

*Exit* ANDREW *and* SANDY *hurriedly, followed by the* DOCTOR.

SPOTTISWOODE Damn ye, John Ogilvie. Damn ye!

*Exit* SPOTTISWOODE.

53

# ACT TWO

## SCENE ONE

*About a month later. Ogilvie's quarters in Spottiswoode's
Castle in Glasgow. As the scene opens,* OGILVIE *is discovered
sitting on the bed reading a book. He looks up from his
reading, closing his eyes, committing a passage to memory.
The high-spirited laughter of a woman is heard off.* OGILVIE
*lays the book aside, frowning, rises to his feet. Enter* ANDREW,
*and, sweeping in behind him,* LADY RACHEL SPOTTISWOODE.
*A tall, handsome woman, she is dressed in a floor-length cloak
and is slightly tipsy, she keeps her arms under the cloak
folded across her chest, and glances about the room with a
rather exaggerated inquisitiveness.*

ANDREW *(grumpily)* Faither, ye hae a visitor. The Leddy Rachel
Spottiswoode.

*Looking rather uncertain,* OGILVIE *steps forward, inclining his
head in the merest suggestion of a bow.*

OGILVIE *(guardedly)* Madam, this is an unlooked-for pleasure.

RACHEL *gives a slight nod and moves past* OGILVIE, *downstage
and across, speaking as she does so.*

RACHEL Weill, Faither, this is hardly what I'd been led to
expect. *(She stops one step away from the end of the bed
and turns to address* OGILVIE *direct.)* Ye seem to be byordnar
comfortable here. They maun be treating ye better nou nor
they did when ye were in Embro!

OGILVIE *(pleasantly)* Madam, it is still . . .

RACHEL Is that richt, Andro? Ye'll hae been tellt to treat the

55

Faither a wee thing kinder here in Glesca nor ye did in Embro?

ANDREW  That's no for me to say, m'leddy.

RACHEL  *(giggles)*  Andro's no very pleased wi me, Faither. Are ye, Andro?

ANDREW  No my place to be pleased or displeased, m'leddy.

RACHEL  Och, wad ye listen to him, Faither? It's my husband, ye see. He's feart the Airchbishop'll get to ken that I've come to see ye!

ANDREW  He's shair tae, m'leddy. And *he'll* no be pleased.

OGILVIE *is looking distinctly unhappy by this time.*

OGILVIE  In that case, madam, perhaps it would be better . . .

RACHEL  Och, Faither Ogilvie, dinna you start! There's nae need to fash about John. I ken weill enough hou to handle *him.* I'll tell him myself — in my ain guid time. Andro, as I was just this minute passing the servants' quarters, I've a notion I heard the sound of merriment and conviviality. *(Flatly.)* I suggest that ye go and get yourself a drink.

ANDREW  *(hardly able to contain his outrage)*  I am on duty, m'leddy.

RACHEL  *(irritably)*  Aw, Andro, dinna you be sic an auld fash! *(Smiles with mischief.)* Faither Ogilvie's a braw-looking cheil richt enough — but he's a man o the cloth and a perfect gentleman, I'm shair. I don't suppose that there's the slightest chance that my honour will be in an danger whatsoever!

ANDREW  *(growling)*  Madam . . .

RACHEL  Andro, that's enough! Dinna argue. Dae what I tell ye. Away ye go! Shoo!

*Reluctantly, glowering at them both,* ANDREW *takes his leave.* OGILVIE *watches him leave somewhat helplessly.*

OGILVIE  Well, madam — would you care to take a seat?

OGILVIE *goes to take the chair from the desk.* RACHEL *steps over to the bed and sits herself down on it.*

56

RACHEL   That's very kind of ye, Faither.

*Perplexed,* OGILVIE *sits down on the chair himself.*

OGILVIE   Well! *(Pauses.)* I'm afraid that I'm unable to offer
you any kind of refreshment.

RACHEL *laughs and rises. She throws back her cloak to reveal
that she has been holding a bottle and two goblets, hiding
them presumably from Andrew.*

RACHEL   No need for apologies, Faither! I brocht my ain!

*She places the bottle and the goblets on the table, and, slipping
off her cloak, throws it on to the bed.* OGILVIE *rises to his feet.*
RACHEL *uncorks the bottle and begins to pour.*

RACHEL   Say when, Faither.
OGILVIE   That will be sufficient madam.

RACHEL *hands him the goblet and pours out a drink for herself.*

RACHEL *(grins)*   Here, I wonder what Mistress Calder and the
ither douce leddies o Glesca toun'd say, gin they could see me
nou? On my lane wi a man — a Catholic priest! — sipping
wine at this time o the nicht! Tut, tut, tut! *(Confidentially,
coming closer to him).* But then Faither Ogilvie, Mistress
Calder and the ither douce leddies o Glesca toun consider me
a harlot and a tippler in any case — so we'll no worry about
them, eh?

*She moves away from him and takes up her seat on the bed.*

OGILVIE   Well, Lady Spottiswoode — your very good health!
RACHEL *(raising her glass)*   And your's, Faither! *(Takes a sip.)*
Tell me — are ye keeping better nou?
OGILVIE   Oh yes! Yes, I've quite recovered from my *(pauses)*
my experience in Edinburgh.

RACHEL   That's fine, then.

OGILVIE *nods and pauses for an instant.*

OGILVIE   Tell me, my lady, what can I do for you? *(Smiles guardedly.)* I take it you've not come to interrogate me?

RACHEL *laughs.*

RACHEL   Hits, na, Faither. I ken nocht o sic maitters! I wadnae ken where to start! Just a wee social visit, that's aa! There's been sic a lot o clash about the toun anent the ongoings o Faither John Ogilvie that I thocht — ach, I had a notion to come and see ye, that's aa! *(Pauses.)* Efter the morn's morn, I michtna get the chance.
OGILVIE *(warily)* No. No. That's true.
RACHEL   Aye! *(Changing the subject.)* They tell me, Faither, that ye left Scotland when ye were nae mair nor a laddie?
OGILVIE   That's correct. I've spent most of my life on the Continent. I only returned last year.
RACHEL   Shairly . . . it maun hae been a thocht to come back?

OGILVIE *pauses a minute before answering, moving away from her downstage.*

OGILVIE   I have a vocation to serve, madam. It is not for me to be afraid of the conditions in which I must serve it.
RACHEL *(smiling)* Dinna mistake me, Faither. That's no what I meant. I was just thinking that Scotland — the place and the folk — maun seem unco strange til ye after aa this time.
OGILVIE *(faintly surprised)* Strange? No. No, not really. I was happy enough in Europe, but Scotland, after all, is my native land — I am no foreigner here!

RACHEL   Mmm. *(Change of subject.)* And did ye manage to see your family?
OGILVIE   My family? *(Suspicious of the question, pauses before*

58

*replying.)* Yes. Yes. I paid a short visit to Banff shortly after I arrived.

RACHEL *(pleasantly)* Oh, they'd be pleased to see ye!

OGILVIE *(laughs bitterly)* Pleased? No, madam, they were hardly pleased!

RACHEL *(rising in concern)* Were they no? But shairly your faither . . .

OGILVIE My father! *(Laughs again.)* My father — and my step-mother and all the rest of them — are heretics! Surely you don't imagine that they'd kill any fatted calves for me?

RACHEL *sits down on the edge of the desk.*

RACHEL Och, I'm no sae shair! Bluid's thicker nor water when aa's said and done!

OGILVIE Water perhaps, madam! Other elements are made of sterner stuff. *(Sighs and walks towards her.)* Look, my lady. My father was asked to make a choice — years ago — between his title and his land on the one hand and his faith on the other. Well you know the choice he made. And if he were asked to make a similar choice — between his property and his blood — which do you think he'd choose?

RACHEL *drains her goblet.*

RACHEL Puir Johnnie! Puir, puir Johnnie Ogilvie! No had much o a homecoming, have ye, son?

OGILVIE *resumes his seat.*

OGILVIE *(with irony)* It certainly has left a lot to be desired!

RACHEL Still, your faither maunnae hae been sae bad! I mean, ye'd shairly hae been a heretic yourself gin he hadnae sent ye . . . .

OGILVIE *rises angrily from his seat.*

OGILVIE Oh that! That, madam, is the greatest irony of all! It was the dying wish of my mother — my real mother, that is — that I should be given a Catholic education. That desire

59

was never honoured until my father married my step-mother — the Lady Douglas — and she saw the opportunity to rob me of my heritage — to seize the title and the property that should be rightfully mine and give them to her own bastard brats! Well, very soon now, I shall be given a greater title — and believe me, madam, there's none of them will have any part in that!

RACHEL *lays her goblet aside thoughtfully.*

RACHEL  Faither, d'ye ken wha ye put me in mind o? Wullie Scott.

OGILVIE *looks puzzled.*

RACHEL  Och, it's an auld tale. There was this laddie in the Borders — Wullie Scott was his name. A cattle thief. Naethin byordnar in that, of course — they're aa cattle-thieves in the Borders, ye ken. Anyway. Wullie was reivin the kye o a man cried Murray — and Murray keppit him at it. In the normal wey o things, Murray wad hae hinged Wullie Scott and that wad hae been that. But it seems that Murray had a problem. He had a dochter — an ill-faured bitch bi the name of Meg — muckle-moued Meg they cried her — and he couldna get onybody to mairry her and take her aff his hands. So he tellt Wullie, he said "See here, Scott. I'll gie ye the choice. Ye can hing — or ye can mairry my dochter. What's it to be?" Wullie took ae look at muckle-moued Meg — and he says "I'll hing!"

OGILVIE  *(huffily)* I fail to see the analogy, madam. I am no criminal.

RACHEL  I didnae say ye were, Faither.

*Enter* ANDREW. *He sees the bottle on the desk and eyes* RACHEL *with suspicion.*

RACHEL  Ah, it's yourself, Andrew. Aye, I suppose I'd better awa. *(She picks up her cloak and takes it over to* ANDREW.)

60

We hae sic a feck o visitors the nou — I'd better go and do my hostess. *(She hands the cloak to* ANDREW, *who holds it for her.)* Thank ye kindly for the refreshment. *(She indicates the bottle and winks at* OGILVIE.) It's been grand talking to ye.

OGILVIE  Likewise, madam.

RACHEL  I trust it'll aa go weill for ye at the trial the morn.

OGILVIE *shrugs.* RACHEL *turns to go, then stops.*

RACHEL  Oh, by the way, Faither. I never tellt ye the end o the tale. Wullie Scott didnae hing, Naw. He thocht about it and decided that discretion was the better pairt o valour. I heard tell that Meg was a guid enough wife till him and that, in time, he even learned to love her.

OGILVIE  Madam, I could never learn to love heresy

RACHEL *(smiles)* Faither, I fear ye dinna take my meaning yet! Guid nicht wi ye!

*Exit* RACHEL *and a relieved* ANDREW. OGILVIE *watches them go, puzzled.*


## SCENE TWO

*The courtyard of the Castle later that night.* WILL, *on guard duty, walks back and forward thoughtfully, holding his spear over his shoulder. He hears a step and comes to the alert.*

WILL  Whoa! Stop richt there, whaever ye are!

THE DOCTOR *steps out of the shadows.*

DOCTOR  It's aaricht, Wullie. It's just myself!

WILL *relaxes.*

WILL  Doctor! Ye gied me a wee gluff there! Ye're shairly out of yer bed late the nicht, are ye no?

*They approach each other in a friendly manner.*

61

DOCTOR  Aye! Just canna get to sleep, Wull! I keep thinkin about the trial the morn.

WILL  *(nodding sadly)* Aye!

DOCTOR  Tell me, Wullie . . . what d'ye think the outcome'll be?

WILL  O the trial?

DOCTOR  Aye.

WILL  That's no for me to say, Doctor. Tae tell ye the truth, I'll no even be there. I'll no be on duty.

DOCTOR  Aye, but ye've shairly some idea! Will they hing him, d'ye think?

WILL *pauses, looks at the Doctor a trifle guardedly, turns away.*

WILL  It looks like it, doctor. Aye. It shairly looks like it!

DOCTOR  Mmm. It strikes me ye wadna be aathegither happy about that, Wullie.

WILL *turns to him suspiciously.*

WILL  What d'ye mean bi that?

DOCTOR  *(innocently)* Naethin! Just that Faither Ogilvie and yourself seem to get on sae weill thegither that I'd hae thocht . . .

WILL  Ogilvie's a prisoner. I'm a gaird. Naethin chynges that!

DOCTOR  Na? That's no what I heard.

WILL  Aye, and whit did ye hear?

THE DOCTOR *smiles.*

DOCTOR  I'm no shair if I can say, Wullie. It concerns a patient o mine, ye see. It michtna be ethical for me to tell *onybody* what I ken. Still, a doctor's no the same as a priest, is he? Whiles, a doctor micht feel it's his duty to betray a professional confidence . . .

WILL  *(shaking his head)* I'm no wi ye, doctor. I've no got a clue o what ye're talkin about!

DOCTOR  I'm talkin about a patient o mine — a man cried
Mayne. John Mayne. Ken wha I mean?

WILL *(shocked rigid)* Oh!

DOCTOR  Aye. Oh Wullie, ye've been an awfy silly laddie!

WILL  I didna mean ony hairm! It was just a wheen letters for
his freins — his faither and his brithers and that — just tae
let them ken hou he was! There was nae hairm . . .

DOCTOR *goes to him and lays his hand on his shoulder.*

DOCTOR  Of course no! Of course there wasna! Still, gin the
bishop was to find out . . . (WILL *looks alarmed.)* Aw dinna
fash, Wullie! Dinna fash! I'll no say a word. Like I said, it
wadna be ethical . . .

WILL *(relieved)* Thanks a lot, doctor! I'll no . . .

THE DOCTOR *looks about him before drawing a yellow parchment from the inside of his coat.*

DOCTOR  Only there's a wee complication. Ane of Faither
Ogilvie's brithers has sent him a reply!

WILL *backs away from* THE DOCTOR.

WILL  Naw! No chance!

DOCTOR  What for no, Wullie? I mean, in for a penny . . .

*Enter* WAT, *none too sober.*

WAT  What the hell's gaun on here?

*Both* WILL *and* THE DOCTOR *are terrified.*

DOCTOR  Oh! It's yersel, Wattie! *(Pauses uncertainly for a
moment.)* I've just brocht this message round for the bishop.
Wullie here seems to think it's owre late in the day to bother
him wi it *(goes to put the paper back in his pocket)* but it
doesna maiter. It'll keep til the morn.

WAT *steps up to* THE DOCTOR *suspiciously and puts his hand out.*

WAT   See's it here!
DOCTOR   It's aaricht, Wat. I tellt ye . . .

WAT *snatches the parchment from his hand.*

WAT   I'll just tak a wee look at it just the same!

THE DOCTOR *turns away, very frightened.* WAT *unfolds the parchment and gazes at it for a few moments without expression. He looks up at* WILL.

WAT   What's the maitter wi this? Eh? Naethin the maitter wi this! See, you take it, gie it tae the bishop the morn. *(Turns to* THE DOCTOR.*)* Save ye a trip back, eh doctor? *(Turns back to* WILL.*)* See? Simple! Nae bother! *(Burps and claps* WILL *on the shoulder.)* I'm awa tae my bed!

WAT *moves off, then stops suddenly, turns slowly and looks at both of them suspiciously, shrugs as if he couldn't care less, then exits.* THE DOCTOR *heaves a huge sigh of relief.*

DOCTOR   Right! I think I'd better get awa nou, Wullie . . .

WILL *strides over to him.*

WILL   Just a second, doctor. *(Holds up the document.)* I'll deliver this. I've nae option nou — sae I'll gie it tae the Faither. But I'm thinkin that you want tae be grateful, doctor, that nane o us can read.

*Without another word,* THE DOCTOR *makes a hurried exit.* WILL *puts the parchment inside his tunic.*

64

## SCENE THREE

*About a month later. Spottiswoode's study in the Castle of the Archbishop of Glasgow. It is a well-furnished, comfortable room, the most dominating features of which are; on the right a writing desk and chair, in the centre a large fireplace with comfortable chairs on either side, on the left a small table with a decanter, water and goblets. It is well past midnight and the fire has died.* SPOTTISWOODE *sits on the left of the fireplace, a book in one hand and a goblet of wine in the other. He sighs and, laying the book aside on his lap, takes a sip of the wine. His wife,* LADY RACHEL SPOTTISWOODE, *dressed in a nightgown and carrying a candle, enters from the right.*

RACHEL *(reprovingly)* John! Are ye wyce, man? For heaven's sake, what ails ye? Ye should be in your bed!

SPOTTISWOODE *looks up at her, shakes his head and sighs.*

SPOTTISWOODE *(absently, almost defensively)* I hae been reading the epistles of the apostle Paul.
RACHEL *(sarcastically)* Oh. I see. Are ye to be examined in them then? — the morn's morn — that ye maun bide up aa nicht in preparation?
SPOTTISWOODE *(with a faint smile)* Woman, your wit is sour.

RACHEL *comes forward and places her candle on the mantlepiece.*

RACHEL I ken. It's the time of nicht — and the sair trial of haeing sic a husband as I hae.

*She sits down opposite him.*

SPOTTISWOODE *(still smiling, rises and takes his goblet over to the drinks table.)* Hae I been sic a bad husband to ye, lass?
RACHEL *(turning in the chair to smile at him)* No, John. No. Ye ken better than to speir that. But there was a time when ye'd

65

tell me aathing — a time when ye'd bring aa your sair bits to
me.

SPOTTISWOODE  And do ye think that time has gane?

RACHEL  It looks like it, John. It shairly looks like it. St. Paul,
it would seem, has mair to offer in the way of comfort than
I.

SPOTTISWOODE *laughs loudly.*

SPOTTISWOODE  Rachel, there can be smaa comfort for me
in these times we live in. The office I hold in our Kirk is
hardly a comfortable ane! Will ye tak a cup of wine with
me m'lady?

RACHEL  Dearie me. *(Sighs.)* Just a small one please, John!

SPOTTISWOODE  *(grinning)* For the stomach's sake?

RACHEL  Aye.

*As* SPOTTISWOODE *pours the drinks, the smile leaves* RACHEL'S
*face and she becomes apprehensive. She turns away from
him.*

RACHEL  John — I went to see John Ogilvie the nicht.

SPOTTISWOODE  *(turning, astounded)* You — what?

RACHEL  I went to see John Ogilvie the nicht.

SPOTTISWOODE  Certes, woman! Whiles ye go past it! What
would Mistress Calder and the leddies o the congregation
. . .

RACHEL  *(with a wave of her hand)* P-y-e-e-h!

SPOTTISWOODE  P-y-e-e-h yourself! Rachel! What in creation
garred ye do a thing like thon! Ogilvie has set this toun on
fire! If it is kent — and certes, it will be kent! — that
Spottiswoode's wife . . . *(Hands her the goblet.)* I do not
ken where ye got the gumption!

RACHEL  *(taking the goblet)* Weill — I maun admit to being a
wee thing leerie about it myself — so I took a rather large
glass of this before I went. So they'll maist likely let on that
I was fou at the time!

66

SPOTTISWOODE *is about to take his seat. He turns on her, fuming and speechless. Looking at her, his temper fades and he smiles and shakes his head hopelessly.*

SPOTTISWOODE  Rachel, oh Rachel! What am I to do with ye?

RACHEL *(seriously)* What am I to do with you, John? I'm sorry if I've offended or upset ye by going to see Ogilvie — but I'd hae thocht myself a sorrier wife gin I had stayed away! John, d'ye no understand? I had to try to discover what it was about this man that was bothering you.

SPOTTISWOODE *(irritably)* Bothering me! Huh! It's no Ogilvie that bothers me!

RACHEL  Is it no? I'm no so sure! John, ye've no been yourself this while past — ill-tempered, growling and snarling aa owre the place, biding up gey near aa nicht, tossing and turning when ye do come to your bed . . . Na, na, my mannie, ye'll na tell me that it's no John Ogilvie that's bothering ye! This aa started on the very day he was arrested! Your bad humour started then. I had a notion to speak with the man that had put ye in sic a humour! So I went to see him.

SPOTTISWOODE  And are ye any the wiser?

RACHEL  I am not! I fail to see what there is to worry ye about this man! I canna help but feel sorry for him, but he's a wrong-headed fool! He micht be a cliver fool, but he's a fool just the same.

SPOTTISWOODE  D'ye tell me that, woman? A clever fool?

RACHEL  Ye needna laugh! Ye ken fine what I mean! The man has faith enough, I daresay! Faith of a kind — but is it the Christian faith? I beg leave to doubt it. I jalouse that even a papist micht beg leave to doubt it! That man cares for nobody but himself — his ain hurts and grievances! And how can he hae any sympathy with the concerns and conditions of ordinary folk? [He kens nocht about them. He has charm enough to spare and a braw sharp tongue — he'd make a bonnie courtier no doubt.] What does he ken o the sufferings

67

o Scotland? He maybe kens principle and argument. He kens nocht o flesh and blood!

SPOTTISWOODE   Principle is necessary, m'dear, in any undertaking — and so is argument. Flesh and blood survive and flourish on the guid maintenance of baith. *(Gets to his feet thoughtfully and walks about.)* What troubles me in this matter is no Ogilvie's faith — I have never doubted nor grudged him that for an instant. He is a man of great faith, of great courage — and of not inconsiderable intellect. Really, Rachel, John Ogilvie is a maist byordnar man. I wish we had a few like him in our Kirk. [Paul tells us — as ye weill ken — that every man should bide the way he was when God called him. I cannot blame Ogilvie for his faith — in his own way, he is as true to his principles as, in his place, I would hope and pray to be to mine.]

RACHEL   Aye. Maybe. But ye ken as weill as I do that there is mair to this than John Ogilvie's faith! Since Paul appears to be in favour the nicht, I would commend to you the advice given by Paul to the Romans anent their responsibilities to the authorities of the State!

SPOTTISWOODE   *(shaking his head irritably)* Oh it's no that, Rachel! It's no that, it's no that!

RACHEL   Weill what is it then?

SPOTTISWOODE   Ye ken what men say about me — and what they said about your faither?

RACHEL   *(hotly)* And you ken me weill enough to ken that I do not care a docken for what men say. My faither stood fast against the papes — and against the presbyterians! You have done the same and I'm proud of ye baith! What time of day is this to be bothering about what men say?

SPOTTISWOODE   Rachel, I am a man of the cloth! It is my business to take tent of what men say. And they say that we were bocht — that we served the King no out of conviction but for the stipend.

RACHEL   Och, John. Ye ken that's no true.

SPOTTISWOODE   Aye! Aye! But d'ye no understand? [We were taking a gamble — your father and myself and the others

— we were taking a gamble with our own guid names, with our reputations.] We kent that it would take time but what we were ettling to effect was a reconciliation — we thocht and gif the Catholics could bend a wee bit and the presbyterians could bend a wee bit, we could bring them aa intil ae strang kirk. Ae kirk in Scotland and peace in the land!

RACHEL   Aye. That's what ye've aye wanted.

SPOTTISWOODE   It was the king's plan but it was us who had to carry it out — [it was men like your faither and me who had to take the gamble.] We kent that it would be a gey hard trauchle. A hard ane and a lang ane — your faither died still trauchling. [But we kent anaa that it was the only way.] And nou *(sighs)* nou we are going to spoil it aa. The morn's morn John Ogilvie will be tried and condemned and the haill thing — years of work — will aa be up in the air!

RACHEL   But John — it's no siccar yet that Ogilvie's to hing!

SPOTTISWOODE   Is it no! Losh woman, ye ken yourself — ye have seen Ogilvie, ye have spoken to him. Is it no obvious what he's after? He pants after the martyr's croun like a dog at a bitch! And they'll gie it to him, thae men that you tell me no to take tent of!

RACHEL   Och, John!

SPOTTISWOODE   Oh aye, they will. Since we came back from Edinburgh, John Ogilvie's name has been on every lip. Gif — no. — *When* he mounts the gallows, the Scottish Catholic community'll take him to their hearts and there will be blood. It'll be war aa owre again! [As for Ogilvie, he'll hae got what he socht, what he returned to Scotland for. Glory, Rachel, Glory and a place in the bloody history of our country! What does he care if the rivers of Scotland run black with the blood of her people, as long as he gets his glory!]

RACHEL   But John, that's no your wyte . . .

SPOTTISWOODE   Did I say it was? Woman, d'ye no understand yet? I hae given everything — my capabilities, my intellect, my honour and my — *oor* guid name — everything to ae single course of action. And the morn's morn, I maun sit doun in that court yonder and watch aa the work that I hae

69

done — and, what's worse — the work I micht hae done
being brocht doun and connached by ane fushionless fanatic!

RACHEL *(going to him)* John, John, my love, ye're making owre
muckle of this! *(Sighs.)* Ye said one true thing anent Ogilvie
— he's a byordnar man. There's no mony'd have stood what
he's stood — I ken what ye did to him in Embro, John — and
if he wants his martyrdom, he's surely earned it. But it'll be
an empty thing, folk'll forget aa about it in no time! Hing
him, John, hing him and ye'll never see his like again!

SPOTTISWOODE Will I no? *(Breaks away from her.)* I'm no
sure. Oh gin I just had the power, gin I could just get him
to listen! Gin I could persuade him! Persuade him to change
his mind . . .

RACHEL *(with an empty laugh)* Recant? Fegs John, he'll never
do that!

SPOTTISWOODE Gin he doesna, I'm feared. Gin he doesna I'm
feared that I'll be hinging him again and again and again.
Owre and owre and owre and owre! Martyrs are a queer-like
breed, Rachel — they hae a way of turning into saints. Saints!
Saint John Ogilvie — can ye no imagine it? Oh Rachel, I
look intae that young man's een and I see a dream — a
dream that is alowe with a bitter hatred. And it is a hatred
that he has never learned — it is a hatred that he has only
dreamed. Oh God! Rachel, how does a man learn sic hatred
— how can a man learn to dream sic dreams?

RACHEL *(quietly)* John, I'm sure I dinna ken.

SPOTTISWOODE No more do I, love, no more do I. *(Savagely.)*
but, shair as daith, I'd better learn! I'd better learn gin my
work in Scotland is to mean ocht ava! For I hae a dream of
my own Rachel, [I hae a dream of my own! Christ's sheep
maun aa be brocht thegither in ae fauld! *(Stops and smiles
a little at his own emotion.)* Paul again, Rachel. Gin we dinna
aa eat thegither at the same table, there will be some wha
maun gang hungry — while ithers get fou! I want a Kirk
in Scotland that will serve aa men.] I want a Kirk in Scotland
that will bring Catholic and Protestant thegither in the ae
faith, in the ae life; I want peace in the land and britherhood

70

and guidwill amang aa men — as the Guid Lord aye intended it should be! [That is *my* dream, Rachel, a dream that is biggit nocht on hatred but — I pray to God! — on love!]

RACHEL Ogilvie can never change that, John.

SPOTTISWOODE No, but he can stop the dream from coming true! He can set the clock back twenty years! Ogilvie can change reality — and it is reality that is important, no dreams! That is a lesson we maun learn here in Scotland! *(Gives a bitter laugh.)* D'ye ken what is the maist absurd thing in this haill business? My auld teacher, my auld lecturer here in Glasgow — Andro Melville — preached the doctrine of the Twa Kingdoms. The temporal and the spiritual. D'ye mind? D'ye mind when King Jamie was seventeen year auld and auld Maister Andro took a grip of him by the arm and tellt him he was 'nocht but God's silly vassal'? [Aye, aye. Maister Andro was aye strang for the Lord and against the King!] Nou Andro Melville's in the Tower of London for exactly the same reason that John Ogilvie's doun the stair! Would it no gar ye laugh? Gin it wasna so deathly serious would ye not see the humour? Melville, wha railed against the 'Harlot of Rome' and Ogilvie wha cries 'damn aa heretics' with geynear every second breath, are both facing death for geynear the exact same reason. Catholic and Protestant could aye unite better in death than they could in life! [But where's Scotland aa this time — where's the sheep that we were aa tellt to feed? They're aa starving to death!]

RACHEL *(thoughtfully)* John, d'ye mind if I tell ye something?

SPOTTISWOODE Woman, I'd like fine to see the day when I could stop you!

RACHEL You're a clever foo anaa! Ye are. Oh I'm no complaining! Ye hae great faith, great learning, great generosity and great compassion. But ye've barely enough imagination to fill this cup!

SPOTTISWOODE Woman, what time o day is this . . .

RACHEL Na, na, na, na, na! Just you haud on and leave me have my say! Ye're sitting there, raxing yourself to daith, biding up aa nicht, pouring owre puir auld Paul looking for

71

some divine answer to your predicament — and aa the time, there's a simple solution to the hail affair staring ye in the face gin ye only had the gumption to take a look at it!

SPOTTISWOODE  There is, is there? And what is that, woman?

RACHEL *goes to the mantlepiece and retrieves her candle.*

RACHEL *(turning to him with the candle in her hand)* Ye're siccar that he'll be condemned the morn?

SPOTTISWOODE  As siccar as I'm standing here.

RACHEL  And ye'll keep him in thon cell there, with a lock on the door and an armed guard ootbye?

SPOTTISWOODE  Aye.

RACHEL  So. Send the guard awa. Unlock the door. What would ye think of that gin you were Ogilvie?

SPOTTISWOODE  Ye think he'd run.

RACHEL *(going slowly to the door)* Ogilvie's young — he's time yet to be a martyr. *(Grins.)* And I ken what Andro Melville would do in he's place! *(Sweeping out.)* Come awa to your bed!

SPOTTISWOODE, *bewildered, gazes at her departing presence.*


## SCENE FOUR

*The following day in the late afternoon. The armoury at Spottiswoode's Castle in Glasgow. It is a roughly furnished but rather cosy room which the soldiers use as a sort of common room in their off-duty periods. There is a rack of spears along the length of the back wall and, in front of this, a long low table with a number of stools all about it.* WILL *is seated at one end of the table, polishing his helmet and* ANDREW *is at the other, sharpening his sword with a whetstone.* WILL'S *sword and* ANDREW'S *helmet lie on the table. They talk as they work.*

72

WILL  Andro?

ANDREW  Aye?

WILL  Were you ever mairrit?

ANDREW  *(laughing)*  Naw, no me!

WILL  Whit for no?

ANDREW  Oh, a lot o reasons!  Never kent a lassie I fancied enough — at least, I never fancied a lassie that fancied me! *(Looks at* WILL *thoughtfully.)* Thinkin aboot it yersel like?

WILL  Aye. I'd hae tae get oot o here . . .

ANDREW  Oh aye! Sodgerin's nae life for a mairrit man!

WILL  . . . but I'm no worried aboot that. I was thinking o packin it in onywey. Nae offence and aa that, Andro, but I dinnae want tae end up like you and Sandy — or, worse yet, like Wattie.

ANDREW  Well, it's up tae yersel, son.

WILL  Aye. Andro, the Faither says I cannae get mairrit — no really mairrit — gin I dinnae get mairrit in a Catholic kirk.

ANDREW  Haw, ye dinnae want tae listen tae the Faither, Christ! He's said a lot, has he no, and see whaur it's got him.

WILL  Aye but — look Andro, gin the Faither hings, there's likely tae be ructions. There micht even be a war! And if the papes were tae win, whaur would that leave me?

ANDREW  Whaur would that leave ony o us? A lot of things can happen in a war, Wullie. Ye micht never see the end o it for one!

WILL  Aye, but if I did! That would mean that I'd hae to be a pape afore I could get mairrit! If the papes won like?

ANDREW  *(laying down the sword and looking at him)* Wullie, ye're a chynged laddie, dae ye ken that? Ye're an awfy chynged laddie. Jist a few short months syne ye were aa for burnin every pape in sicht! D'ye mind when we brocht Ogilvie in? D'ye mind whit ye were wantin tae dae tae him then?

WILL  I didnae ken the Faither then; I didnae ken — I had nae idea o hou mony folk in Scotland were still papes at hert.

Aw, I'm no one o them, dinnae fash yersel aboot that! **But I**
hae tae look oot for mysel and for —

ANDREW  For yer maw?

WILL  For the lassie that I want tae mairry! There are places
in Scotland whaur the ministers hae tae tak swords intil the
pulpits wi them! Aye! Gin the papes were tae get back . . .

ANDREW  Wullie, I'll set yer mind at rest! The papes arenae
comin back, son. The papes are never comin back!

WILL  *(sceptically)*  I dinnae ken hou ye can be sae shair.

ANDREW  Dae ye no? Weill, I'll tell ye. The papes arenae comin
back because the gentry — Faither Ogilvie's ain kind —
'll never let them. Christ, the reason — I winnae say the only
reason — why the papes got kicked oot of the country in the
first place was so's thae buggers could get their hauns on the
ferms and the big hooses and aa the property and treisour
that belanged tae the Roman kirk. Ye'll no tell me that they're
gonnae hand aa that back for a daft-like thing like religion?
*(Laughs.)* Ye'll no tell me that Tam o the Cougait's gonnae
gie back Melrose Abbey so that the papes can stop a laddie
like you frae gettin mairrit!

WILL  *(nodding, still troubled)*  Mebbe ye're richt, Andro, mebbe
ye're richt. Still, gin the Faither hings . . .

WILL *is interrupted by the excited entrance of* WAT *and* SANDY.

WAT  That's it, then. The pape's tae hing!

WILL  When?

SANDY  On the tenth. Jesus Andro, ye should have seen this!
*(*WILL *picks up his sword and helmet and leaves the room.)*
Here, whit's the maitter wi the boy?

ANDREW  Never mind him. He's got a lot tae learn, that's aa.

SANDY  Aye, Him and the Faither's been gettin gey chief this
last wee while. He'll be upset bi the news.

WAT  *(taking the seat that* WILL *has vacated)*  Aye and he's
no the only ane either! Ye want tae have seen the greetin in
the coort the day, Andro — eh, Sandy? No aa weemen either!

SANDY  *(coming round and taking his seat beside* ANDREW*)*  Aye,

Ogilvie's taen the trick wi them richt enough. **Wadnae mind**
bettin there'll be a puckle trouble nou!

WAT  B'Christ there will! You jist watch! See, that's the thing
wi papes — they worm awa intae people, turn them against
their ain kind. They should hae hung that bugger months
syne! See whit he's done tae young Wullie. He was a guid
laddie that, at one time. But see nou? I'll tell ye this — if
there is trouble, I'll be awfy careful aboot turnin my back on
him. In my opinion . . .

ANDREW *(angrily)* That's the trouble wi aa you buggers — ye're
aa fu o yersels, ye've aa got opinions! Weill, I've an opinion
anaa! *(Picks up his sword and hits the table with it.)* That's
it there! And if there is trouble, Wattie, and I see you turnin
yer back on *onybody,* I'll soon enough gie ye my opinion,
son! You bet I will!

WAT *glares back hatefully at* ANDREW *but says nothing.*

SANDY  Aye, he will anaa! He will! *(Pause.)* Andro . . .

ANDREW  Aaricht, Sandy. Aaricht. I can see that I'm gonnae
get it aa sooner or later — I can see ye're fair burstin tae
let it aa oot — sae it micht as weill be nou. Whit happened
at the trial?

SANDY *(enthusiastically)*...Weill, Andro, seein ye asked, I'll tell
ye. It was somethin. It was somethin tae see aaricht! Nou,
I'd hae thocht that — efter whit happened in Embro — that
the Faither'd have calmed doun a wee, behaved himself like?
Not a bit of it! My, my, but did he no gie them laldy! I'll
say this for him — he's fit for them aa in a slangin match. Is
that no richt, Wat?

WAT  Oh aye.

SANDY  He said he didnae gie a rotten fig for the jury, that the
judges were aa like flies swarmin roun a lump o shite — weill,
he didnae say shite, bein aa pan-loaf and a priest and that, but
we aa kent whit he meant — he said he wadnae set doun
holy things afore dugs and — tae cap it aa — he tellt the
haill coort that the King was nae mair tae him nor an auld

75

hat! Christ, ye want tae have seen Spottiswoode's face! If looks could kill, there'd be nae need for a hingin!

ANDREW  In ither wards, he pit the raip aroun his ain thrapple! I thocht he wad. *(Stands up and, taking his sword, holds it up to the light and looks along the edge.)* And it's a bluidy waste, d'ye ken that? A man wi he's smeddum and brains could dae a haill lot o guid!

WAT  *(Sneering)* Ye're shairly gettin auld, Andro. Auld and saft! What guid is there in a papish priest? There's owre mony o the fuckers in Scotland as it is!

ANDREW  *(coldly)* He had echt days and nine nichts of pure bluidy hell in Embro. You ken that, torturer, you gave him the maist o it — and he never even looked like breakin! In spite of yer nails and yer mallet and yer clairty wee mind, he never came near tae beggin for mercy! And as far as the law's concerned, bein a papish priest isnae a hingin maitter.

WAT  *(smugly)* But he's no hingin for bein a papish priest! He's hingin for bein a traitor — he wadnae tak the Aith o Allegiance!

ANDREW  Then he should hae got the jile until he did! [Och, it's no for me tae say that he shouldnae be punished — I'm no even sayin that he shouldnae hing! It jist seems tae me that it's a gey donnert thing for a man like Ogilvie, wi aa his smeddum and brains, tae fling his ain life awa like that! ] Ach, whit gars me grue the maist is the fact that aa this argy-bargy is aboot sweet fuck-all! *(Holds the naked sword up before him.)* The haun that hauds this sword has killed mair men nor I hae years o my life — and whit for? Whit some bluidy jyner said or didnae say in Palestine hundreds o years syne! Christ, it gies me the boke tae think o it! *(Looks at WAT.)* You'll mebbe no mind on this, but Sandy will. Back in the year o' 96 . . .

SANDY  Oh aye. I mind aaricht. The seventeenth o September riot. I mind thon aaricht!

ANDREW  The seventeenth o September. In Embro. There was a mob o thousans that day — aa bearin wappins and wantin tae kill the King. And at the heid o them aa was the

76

meenisters. Bruce. Welsh. Black. "For God and the Kirk"
they cried "For God and the Kirk!" And on the ither side
— on the ither side, there was anither mob. And they were
shoutin "For God and the King!" God and the King! The
bluid and the snot ran through the streets o Embro like a
torrent that day!

WAT  Oh. aye. I mind on that that anaa. It was a sair business
richt enough — but it was aa King Jamie's wyte . . .

ANDREW  Oh was it? Aaricht weill, whaur's King Jamie nou?
He's still got his croun on his heid — at least, it's no the same
croun but a bigger ane — and whaurs Robert Bruce? Whaur's
John Welsh? Huh! The King's on his throne and the
meenisters are in their pulpits yet! It's aye the same — the
meenisters and the priests and the high-heid anes'll dae the
argyin and the stirrin up — but when it comes tae the killin
and the deein, weill there's nane o them can lift up the deid
they left on the streets o Embro that day. And they're never
satisfied. When Ogilvie hings we'll hae anither riot, this time
on the streets o Glesca. And it'll no be the meenisters that'll
dae the fechtin or the killin or dein — it'll be you and me
and Sandy and young laddies like Wullie!

WAT  (laughing, quite insensitive to what ANDREW is saying) Be
fair, Andro! Be fair! It'll be Ogilvie anaa!

ANDREW  Aw fine Ogilvie. Ogilvie'll gae til the gallows and hae
his craig stretched — fine for him! That's what he wants,
that's whit he's efter! They'll mak a martyr oot o'm nae
doubt — pent his pictur and hing it up on the Vatican waa!
Great for Ogilvie! But whae'll fecht the battles that he'll
leave ahint him? No John Ogilvie. He's away! (Sighs and
sheaths his sword.) And so am I. Better get back tae work,
back tae the bluidy job!

ANDREW picks up his helmet and walks towards the door
somewhat wearily.

WAT  (Addressing SANDY but really taunting ANDREW) It's like
I was sayin, Sandy. Ye cannae trust thae papes. They get in
aawhere — even here.

ANDREW *stops and considers* WAT *amusedly.*

ANDREW   What's the maitter, Wattie? Ye're shairly no gonnae tell me that ye're worried aboot turnin yer back on me?

WAT   *(rises, walks towards the centre of the room)*   Turnin my back? I made up my mind on that score as far as you were concerned a while syne.

SANDY *rises and moves away from the table, behind* WAT *who is facing* ANDREW *from the middle of the room.*

ANDREW   *(very quietly)*   And what dae ye mean bi that, son?

WAT   I mean that you're a pape — I mean that you're a Pope's man. I mean that I wadnae trust ye as far as I can throw ye!

ANDREW   *(stiffens, goes very quiet)*   I hope you're feelin lucky, son!

WAT   Ha! Listen tae the hard man! I dinnae need luck for you, ye tired auld priest's (SANDY *very quickly draws his sword and prods* WAT *in the back with it)* bastard!

SANDY   *(laughing)*   Ha, ha! Wattie, ye werenae mindin yer p's and q's. I micht be a pape anaa for aa ye ken! Will I disarm him, Andro?

ANDREW   Naw! *(Strides forward and gives* WAT *the back of his hand across the face.)* Ye daft cunt! I micht hae killed you! Comin the haurd-case! You stick tae yer buits and yer mallet and yer nails! Because the next time you try onythin like thon, the best you can hope for is tae be flung in a cell withoot a door in it. D'ye understand?

WATT   *(wiping his cheek where* ANDREW *struck him)*   I micht hae kent that the pair o ye wad hing thegither.

ANDREW   We aa hing thegither! We aa hing thegither — or we aa end up deid! That's the rule, Wattie. For Christ's sake, get it intae yer thick heid and forget aboot papes and protestants and bein feart aboot turnin yer back! We'll forget aboot this — you jist mak shair it disnae happen again, richt? *(WAT makes no answer.)* Richt?

WAT   *(reluctantly)*   Aye.

78

ANDREW *nods and exits.* SANDY *sheaths his sword.* WAT *returns to where he was sitting.*

SANDY  Christ, Wattie, that was a daft-like thing tae try. What got intae ye?

WAT  Ach, I got pissed off wi him! Him and aa that talk aboot the seventeenth o September! Christ, ye'd think the pape's'd never done onything!

SANDY  I'll no argy wi ye, Wattie. But ye're a lucky bugger tae be sittin there the nou. Andro's a haurd man, Wat. He's no lived as lang as he has for naethin. His sword'd have been through your guts afore ye'd got yer ain clear o the scabbard! Jist dinnae try that again, son. I'm warnin ye!

WAT  Aye? Weill maybe . . . *(looks towards the door)* but I still say ye cannae trust thae papish bastards!


## SCENE FIVE

*Ogilvie's room in the Castle on the night of the 9th March 1615. It is slightly more comfortable than his quarters in Edinburgh (inasmuch as there is a small fire) but it is just as barely furnished.* OGILVIE, *dressed completely in white is seated at a table writing. He finishes, sands the paper, folds it and goes to the door and knocks.*

OGILVIE  Will! *(WILL enters.)*

OGILVIE  *(handing WILL the paper)* This is the last. You know where to take it.

WILL  Aye.

WILL *takes the paper from* OGILVIE, *puts it inside his tunic.*

WILL  *(with a sigh and a shake of the head)* Oh Faither, this is the last for me anaa!

79

OGILVIE *gives a speechless, unsteady smile but says nothing. Quickly, somewhat impulsively,* WILL *doffs his helmet and kneels before* OGILVIE. OGILVIE *is taken aback for a second, then smiles and places his hand on* WILL'S *head.*

OGILVIE   Nomine Patris et Filis . . . The Lord bless you and keep you. *(*WILL *gives a small, choked sob.)* Oh Willie. Willie! Arise, my son, arise! *(*OGILVIE *takes him by the shoulders and brings him to his feet, talking to him gently and kindly.)* You must not grieve for me, Will! Do you not remember when I told you — a long time ago — that this is my destiny? Tomorrow my destiny will be fulfilled. Tomorrow — they are going to put a crown of precious stones upon my head! *(He looks at* WILL *inquiringly.* WILL *nods.)* So no tears, boy. Go now. Go and give my messages and my story to my brethren that the world shall know what happened here.

WILL *nods again and turns.* SPOTTISWOODE *enters and stands at the door. Coming face to face with him,* WILL *freezes.*

SPOTTISWOODE   Ye hae secured your prisoner, Wull?
WILL *(shakily)*   Aye aye, m'lord. M'lord . . .
SPOTTISWOODE   Guid. Ye'd best get awa to your bed nou. Ye'll no be wantit again the nicht. *(When* WILL *hesitates.)* Go, boy! It's aaricht!

WILL *goes but stops briefly at the door.*

WILL   Guidby, Faither.
OGILVIE *(quietly, with a kind smile)* Goodbye, Will. Take care!

WILL *leaves.*

OGILVIE *(rather too eagerly when* WILL *has gone)* Will has been very good to me. I am most indebted to you for putting him at my disposal. I have given him some letters for my family, he has promised to see that they are delivered safely . . .

OGILVIE *lets his rather guilty words trickle away into silence.*

SPOTTISWOODE   Family? The Heretics? Ye make a damned poor
liar, John Ogilvie. Did ye ken that?

OGILVIE *(with some heat)* Spottiswoode, I had hoped never to
see you again and do not in the least know what you hope
to gain by coming here tonight! But since you are here —
and will no doubt state your business in due course — I
would thank you to spare me your insults for I am completely
beyond them now!

*Ignoring him,* SPOTTISWOODE *paces the floor a little in
thought.*

SPOTTISWOODE   Tell me, Faither. Did ye hae any success with
the boy?

OGILVIE   Boy? What boy?

SPOTTISWOODE   The laddie! Wullie! Did ye manage to convince
him of the true faith?

OGILVIE   That's for you to find out!

SPOTTISWOODE   Aw, Faither, come on! I'm no going to set
up a new trial at this time of day! I was only voicing a professional interest, that's aa! And gin ye dinnae wish to tell
me, I'll no press ye! *(Pauses.)* Houever, I would be interested
to ken if ye tried. Did ye? Did ye try?

OGILVIE *(taken aback)* As a matter of fact — since you ask
— I didn't. *(Laughs.)* I didn't. I never even thought of it. I
gave him some instruction — Look, Will is no catholic,
believe me when I tell you that! Please do not persecute him
on my account!

SPOTTISWOODE   No, no, no, no, Faither Ogilvie, ye misunderstand me! I'm no interested in the laddie! I ken him for an
honest young man and a loyal and faithful servant! It's you
that interests me, Faither Ogilvie, you! Ye didna try, ye tell
me? Forgive me, Faither — I'll no doubt ye, never fear! —
but I find that a wee thing strange.

OGILVIE   Not all that strange. Right from the start — from

81

the very day I was taken into captivity — I realised that I had to be strong, that I had to raise my voice and shout. I knew that if I did otherwise, I was lost! That is to say, my cause was lost — there was never any hope for me personally and I knew it. I knew that I had to be strong, I expected nothing from my jailers but blows and abuse. I certainly never expected charity.

SPOTTISWOODE  And yet ye got it from Wullie?

OGILVIE  Yes. Yes. I never asked for it, I certainly never begged for it — and yet, without I myself doing anything at all, Will changed — he changed from a rough-tongued, bigoted youth into a warm-hearted and decent fellow man. I do not know how I would have kept my sanity and my courage without him. And I? I gave him nothing! Oh he would occasionally ask me a question about faith or behaviour and I would give him my opinion, — but I did not minister to him. I gave him nothing!

SPOTTISWOODE  Faither Ogilvie. Will is damned. Will is going straight to the fires of hell!

OGILVIE  (outraged)  That's a terrible thing to say!

SPOTTISWOODE  Aye, maybe! But I dinna say it — you do!

OGILVIE  I have never said any such thing!

SPOTTISWOODE  Have ye no? And what have ye been saying this last half-year? You tellt me — in Embro last January — that even the youngest bairn baptised by a presbyterian minister was damned!

OGILVIE  I never said that — I said that he was within the Pope's authority as far as . . .

SPOTTISWOODE  . . . punishment is concerned. I ken. And what if he bides outwith the Pope's authority? What if he never becomes a Catholic? He's damned! You said that, Faither Ogilvie, you believe that! You had the chance to save Wullie's soul — according to your own beliefs — and you threw it away. Ye didna try!

OGILVIE  Do not seek to burden me on the gallows with a lost soul! There are other priests!

SPOTTISWOODE  Aye. There *are* other priests — or will be.

There are episcopalian and presbyterian ministers as well — wha kens? Willie micht weill win to heaven yet! Houever, let us no get into *that* argument! I didna come here the nicht to burden your heart with a lost soul — I came for quite another purpose. *(Very carefully, he pauses to frame his words.)* Faither Ogilvie, when first we met and I speired at ye what had garred ye return to Scotland, ye tellt me — as I mind — that it was to save souls. To 'unteach heresy' was the phrase, as I mind?

OGILVIE    That is correct. That is why I came.

SPOTTISWOODE    Ye haena had muckle success, hae ye?

OGILVIE    Time alone will tell about that.

SPOTTISWOODE    Time? *(Nods.)* Faither, ye are due to hing the morn's afternoon. Ye'll be aware, no doubt, that the courageous — if perverse — manner in which ye hae conducted yourself in the course of the various hearings has attracted a certain popular element, a mob following. And ye will be aware anaa that there is a certain anti-Catholic element in this city. By the morn's nicht, there could be riots. We are expecting riots. We are expecting blood to flow on the streets of Glasgow.

OGILVIE    *(unhappily)* That is not a consideration that I am in a position to entertain.

SPOTTISWOODE    No. But ye will appreciate that as a man of God and as spiritual leader of this community, I am anxious to avoid needless bloodshed?

OGILVIE    I, too, am a man of God, Archbishop — but if there are riots because of me tomorrow night, it will not be the first time that men have spilled blood over religion — nor, I fear, will it be the last. I repeat — I am in no position to think about it.

SPOTTISWOODE    Faither Ogilvie, do you esteem your life a success? Do you feel that there is nothing left for you to achieve?

OGILVIE    If I could serve my faith in the clean air of freedom, there would be a great deal. But if I cannot live without compromising my faith? *(Smiles sadly.)* It is another consideration I am in no position to entertain.

83

SPOTTISWOODE   Your faith? Oh, aye. Nou, there's a question . . . (*Pauses carefully, regards* OGILVIE *thoughtfully.*) Tell me, Faither Ogilvie, what *is* your faith?

OGILVIE (*angrily*)   Surely I have made that plain enough by this time!

SPOTTISWOODE   Ye havena — that's just what I'm saying! Oh, ye've speechified and argued and swaggered and bragged your way throughout this whole affair — but you have just this minute admitted to me that you had the chance to save the soul of one young man from eternal damnation — and that you did not even try! So I want tae ken, John Ogilvie. What *is* your faith?

OGILVIE   I thought you said that you would not burden my heart with a lost soul!

SPOTTISWOODE   Nor will I! For Wullie is my responsibility and his soul is *not* lost — nor will it be while I hae ocht to do with it! So forget about Wullie — what about yourself?

OGILVIE   You want me to recant!

SPOTTISWOODE (*sighs exasperatedly*)   Since you seem to be unable to understand what I mean, let me put it another way. Are you a Christian — or are you a Jesuit?

OGILVIE (*lookes at* SPOTTISWOODE *speculatively for a moment, then suddenly laughs*)   You do! You want me to recant! You want me to save my life by denying my faith!

SPOTTISWOODE (*snorts*)   It's no possible for a traitor to recant. Damn the Pope to hell if ye like, it'll do you no good. But is your lealty to the Society of Jesus mair important than your lealty to Our Lord Himself? Would you live for Christ — or die for Ignatius? That's the question that I'm speiring at you!

OGILVIE   Spottiswoode, I have been condemned to die — but in condemning me, you and your like condemn all our ancestors, all the ancient bishops and kings, all the priests — all that was once the glory of Scotland! Do you not understand that to be condemned with all these old lights is a a matter of gladness and joy for me. God lives, Spottiswoode, posterity lives and the judgment of posterity will not be so corrupt as yours. You call my religion treason . . .

84

SPOTTISWOODE *(snapping)* But what *is* your religion?

OGILVIE  I am a Catholic man and a priest. In that faith I have lived and in that faith I am content to die . . .

SPOTTISWOODE  Rhetoric. Sheer, empty-headed, bloody-minded rhetoric. To put Catholicism before Christianity is bad enough — but no man will ever be condemned to death in Scotland for that! But you put your Jesuitism before your Christianity and your Catholicism! That is why you are going to hang! Certes, Ogilvie, you are an ignorant man! Your ignorance appals me. What do you ken of folk — plain ordinary common Scottish folk! What dou you ken and what do you care that men will kill and die, women will be widowed and bairns will be orphaned because of you and your illbred pride? What do you ken of Scotland — guidsakes man, what garred you return after all these years? Ye canna even speak the language! What do you ken of religion? Oh aye, ye've been well trained and can quote Holy Scripture by the mile — but what is your religion to you? "Feed my sheep" said the Lord — but you hae a gey funny notion of how to feed sheep! You'd feed sheep by killing kings! And that's what it all comes doun to — your religion, I mean. Christianity is a religion of life — the god you serve is a god of daith!

OGILVIE *(stiffly)* In your judgment perhaps. Posterity, as I have said, will take a different view.

SPOTTISWOODE  Posterity! Ha! And what will posterity hold for you?

OGILVIE  It is not important what it will hold for me, but some day we may have a Catholic Scotland again and if my action . . .

SPOTTISWOODE  A Catholic Scotland! There will never be a Catholic Scotland any more than there will be a Presbyterian or Episcopalian Scotland! But that's no important — perhaps some day there'll be a Christian Scotland. And how will posterity judge you then?

OGILVIE *(hotly)* As a man who stood by his principles against the threats and tortures of pagans and unbelievers!

SPOTTISWOODE  D'ye think so? D'ye really think so? What you

85

call your 'principles' will be long-forgotten political issues in less than twenty years time! And then history will see ye as ye really are — the false shepherd who betrayed his flock in the vain hope of winning a martyr's croun!

OGILVIE  And who are you to accuse me of betrayal, you — you Judas! You who betrayed your own cause to the sinful vanity of a decadent and Godless King!

SPOTTISWOODE  I micht hae kent that sooner or later ye wad hae brocht that ane up — but ye needna hae bothered! That charge has been made afore this with greater eloquence than even you can summon — *and* my conscience is clear. I had guid reasons for what I did!

OGILVIE  *(laughing)* Oh, no doubt! Hundreds of reasons for leaving your presbyterian ministry and thousands of reasons for taking on your episcopalian diocese!

SPOTTISWOODE  Certes but you're the sharp ane! You're the sharp ane richt enough. With half a dozen wits as sharp as yours I could chynge Scotland, I could chynge the warld!

OGILVIE  Then it's as well that I'm going to the gallows because you're going straight to hell!

SPOTTISWOODE, *struck dumb with horror, stiffens and balls his fists.* OGILVIE *immediately regrets his words.*

OGILVIE  Pardon me, m'lord. That was not well said. Whatever our intentions, it seems that we always end up shouting at each other. I know that you did not change your church for material gain — and I believe that you know, that you must know in your heart that I am no death worshipper! God knows I do not want to die! I am as in love with life as any man! But there is no way out of my situation — no way at all.

SPOTTISWOODE  There is one way — that's why I'm here the nicht.

OGILVIE  *(hopelessly)* I cannot go back on anything that I've said.

SPOTTISWOODE  There's no need to. The locks hae been removed

86

from aa the doors and my men hae their orders. Gin ye should decide to leave the Castle the nicht, there's nane will detain ye.

OGILVIE *seems about to make some outraged reply, but something in* SPOTTISWOODE'S *expression makes him hold his tongue. Instead, he moves to his chair and sits down wearily.*

OGILVIE   And where do you think I could go? What kind of reception do you think I would receive from my brethren were I to run away at this hour?

SPOTTISWOODE   That would be up to yourself. But ye are yet a young man — young for a priest at any rate. In time . . .

OGILVIE   Yes, I suppose I might be able to live it down. I would be able to preach again — might even be able to . . . some day . . . to come back to Scotland. *(He glances enquiringly at Spottiswoode.)*

SPOTTISWOODE   *(doubtfully)*   Weill . . .

OGILVIE   No. No. I would never be able to come back to Scotland.

OGILVIE *sits brooding in his chair, his head turned away from* SPOTTISWOODE. *There is a set of rosary beads lying on the table. Absently,* OGILVIE *reaches over and picks them up, laying them on his lap.* SPOTTISWOODE *senses that he is tempted by the offer of freedom.*

SPOTTISWOODE   *(with passion)*   Ogilvie! Save yourself, Ogilvie! Save yourself! In the name of the Lord Jesus Christ, I beseech you . . .

OGILVIE *turns, looks at* SPOTTISWOODE *wordlessly, then looks away.*

SPOTTISWOODE   *(throwing his hands in the air)*   Fare ye weel, Faither Ogilvie. One way or the other, fare ye weel!

SPOTTISWOODE *starts to leave.*

87

OGILVIE (*rising stiffly to his feet*) My Lord Archbishop!
(SPOTTISWOODE *turns expectantly towards him.*) There is just
one thing before you leave.

SPOTTISWOODE Aye?

OGILVIE (*extending his hand*)  I would require your hand.

SPOTTISWOODE *almost responds. He looks at the outstretched
hand and then at* OGILVIE.

SPOTTISWOODE No. No. This is no game, Faither, This is no
game.

SPOTTISWOODE *turns and goes, leaving* OGILVIE *standing with
his hand outstretched. Slowly,* OGILVIE *lets his arm fall to his
side.*


## SCENE SIX

*The hangman's quarters, within sight of the gallows.*
OGILVIE *kneels in prayer, with his rosary wound round his
fingers and his eyes tightly shut.* THE SOLDIERS *stand by
watching him patiently. Their swords are drawn and they
carry shields. In the distance, the sound of drums can be heard.*
SPOTTISWOODE *enters impatiently, followed by* THE HANG-
MAN. *Both check as they see* OGILVIE *at prayer.* OGILVIE
*finishes praying, opens his eyes, and rises unsteadily to his
feet. He sees* SPOTTISWOODE *as he turns.*

OGILVIE My Lord.

SPOTTISWOODE (*quietly*) Ye are ready now? (OGILVIE *nods.*
SPOTTISWOODE *looks about himself in exasperation and says
to no-one in particular.*) Better get on wi't then!

*Exit* SPOTTISWOODE. THE HANGMAN *approaches* OGILVIE *with
bowed head.* OGILVIE *goes to meet him, taking him lightly
by each sleeve.*

88

OGILVIE  Be of good heart, my friend. I have forgiven you already. Will . . .

WILL *turns as he calls.* OGILVIE *goes to him and embraces him.*

OGILVIE  Take care, my son! My time has come. Take care.

WILL, *choked with emotion, turns away.*

OGILVIE  Sandy! Goodbye to you!

SANDY *pumps* OGILVIE'S *hand.*

SANDY  Here's tae ye, Faither. Here's tae ye!
OGILVIE  Wat!

WAT *turns away and spits.*

OGILVIE  Andrew! Can I just say that . . .
ANDREW  *(roughly)* Say naethin, Faither! The time for words is past! *(Prods* THE HANGMAN *with his sword.)* Come on, you! Get on wi't. *(Turns to the other soldiers.)* Right. Sandy and me'll tak it frae here! *(They prepare to move off.)*
WILL  Andro . . .
ANDREW  Aye?
WILL  Can I no come instead o Sandy?

ANDREW *and* SANDY *exchange wise smiles.*

ANDREW  Been on the gallows afore, have ye?
WILL  Naw, but . . .
ANDREW  Then I'm no wantin ye! *(Softer.)* Listen, son. Ye ken there's gonnae be trouble — bound tae be. There's no an awfy lot o room up by the scaffold thonder. Mair nor twa o us and we'd just be gettin in ane another's road. Best leave it tae Sandy and me, son — we're auld hands at this gemme.
SANDY  Aye, Andro's richt, son. You listen tae Andro. Him and me, we've . . .

ANDRO *(to* SANDY*)* You shut up! *(To* THE HANGMAN.*)* Come on! Let's dae the job.

*They are about to move off again, when* OGILVIE *suddenly stops dead and turns to them all.*

OGILVIE Wait! *(Looks pointedly at* ANDREW, *who makes a pained expression.)* I have one last word for you all. If there are any hidden Catholics among you, I would welcome your prayers — but the prayers of heretics I will not have!

ANDREW *explodes with anger.*

ANDREW Get him oot o here!

THE HANGMAN *takes* OGILVIE *by the arm, but* OGILVIE *stands his ground.* ANDREW *comes forward and pushes* OGILVIE *in the chest with his sword hand. Between* THE HANGMAN *and* ANDREW, OGILVIE *is pushed and hauled off the stage, followed by* SANDY.
   WILL *watches them leave anxiously. Unconcerned,* WAT *sheathes his sword.*

WAT He doesnae trust ye, son.

*A huge roar is heard from outside.*

WILL *(sheathing his sword)* What's that?
WAT The auld fella. Andro. I'm sayin he doesnae trust ye.
WILL *(absently)* Aye? Weel, he's richt enough, I suppose.
WAT Aye, ye see, it doesnae dae tae get owre chief wi a prisoner, Wullie. It doesnae dae, son.
WILL Does it no? Weel, Andro kens I'll aye dae the job. He kens he can rely on me.
WAT He does, does he? Huh! That's mair nor I wad dae!
WILL What for no, eh?
WAT Aw, come on, son! Ye're jokin! See ye there the nou

— ye were near greetin! I'm gaun up tae the gallows tae hing a man — wi a big mob like that ane ootby — and the boy that's meant tae be helpin me's greetin like a wean acause the prisoner's tae be hung? Foo! Forget it, son! No danger!

WILL Aye, weel, it wisnae you that was gaun tae the gallows in any case!

WAT So what? What the hell's the odds whae goes up? The thing is, Wullie — ye're no reliable. Ye took up wi that pape and there's nane o us can depend on ye!

WILL Aye, so ye say — but Andro doesna think that! Neither does Sandy. Ach, you, ye dinnae understand onything, you dinnae! I'll no deny I thocht a lot on Faither Ogilvie — but I'm no ashamed o that! He's a guid man . . .

WAT Is he . . .

WILL You shut yer mooth! He's worth ten o you ony day o the week!

WAT Aw, is that right? Weel, listen son, I'll tell ye somethin aboot your precious Faither Ogilvie. He's a crappin bastard! He's got a big yellae streak rinnin aa the wey doun his back!

*A huge roar is heard from outside. They pause as they hear it.*

WAT I ken. I ken Ogilvie's kind weel enough. And I'm tellin you, Wullie . . .

WILL Aw, you get stuffed!

WAT Listen, d'ye want me tae prove it tae ye? I'm a torturer, son — and part o my tredd's kennin when a man's feart and when he's no. I kent he's kind the minute I clapped eyes on him.

WILL Aye, when ye went tae meisure him for the buits!

WAT Aye, he didnae get the buits though, did he? He got somethin worse, I reckon. And I'm no shair but that *that* didnae brak him. I'm no shair but he didnae cough his load tae the Archbishop.

WILL Balls! Whit the hell are they hingin him for then?

*Another huge roar is heard from outside. Again they pause.*

WAT   I dinnae ken. But I ken this; mind when he was in Glesca first, just efter the arrest? What was he like? Eh? Ye ken yersel. Doun in the dungeon amang the rats and aa the shit and filth o the day! A twa-hunner pund wecht chyned til his leg! Aye. And hou's he been this past while? A different story. A wee room o his ain, a table, a chair, a bed, visitors tae see him, buiks tae read, wine tae drink, Lady Spottiswoode . . . Even you have tae admit there's somethin twisted about that!

WILL   There's just the wan thing that's twisted aboot here . . .

WAT   Listen, hou d'ye fancy a wee bet? Eh? Hou d'ye fancy a wee wager that they'll hae tae turn him aff.

WILL   Turn him aff? What's that?

WAT   Shove him aff, ye fule! He'll get tae the tap o the scaffold syne put up a fecht! They'll hae tae gie him the heave!

WILL   Naw! Naw! No chance! No him! Never him!

WAT   Aye, we'll see then, eh? Just you wait! We'll see.

*Enter* SANDY, *running.*

SANDY   *(out of breath)*   Jesus Christ, I never saw anythin like thon in aa my born days!

WAT   What happened, Sandy! Tell us what happened!

SANDY *leans against* WILL *for support. He is out of breath for the duration of his speech.*

SANDY   Aw, wait'll I catch my braith! Lads, I'll tell ye . . . Oh my God!

WILL   What happened, Sandy? What happened?

SANDY   The Faither — he goes up there quite checko, ye ken? Kisses the scaffold — aye, kisses the bluidy scaffold. Then this laddie manages tae get up on the gallows.

WAT   What then?

SANDY   Aw, Andro sorted him aaricht. Nae messin. Boom,

92

boom. Puir laddie. I hope he wasnae thinkin o gettin mairrit.

WILL Never mind him! What about the Faither?

SANDY Ogilvie takes his rosary and he slings it intae the crowd
. . .

WILL Aye, that'd be him right enough.

SANDY Aye, weel, we get him aa tied up and the hangman
takes him up the scaffold. He had a bit o a job o it, what wi
Ogilvie's hands bein ahint his back and that — but onyway,
he gets him up. Ogilvie's chantin awa at this Latin prayer aa
the time. The hangman gets him up — and he says tae him
"Say it, John. Lord have mercy on me. Lord, receive my
soul" and Ogilvie says it "Lord, have mercy on me. Lord,
receive my soul". And then . . .

WAT Aye! Aye! What happened then!

SANDY Aw, Christ I dinnae ken! There was a struggle . . .
the hangman couldnae manage . . . Andro had tae sclim
the ladder and shove the Faither aff!

WAT I tellt ye! I tellt ye! The bastard crapped it at the last!
I tellt ye he was yella, Wullie! I tellt ye! (Slaps one palm
against the other.) Put it there, son! Put it there!

WILL *loses his temper completely and goes for* WAT.

WILL Shut up, you! Shut up, shut up, shut up! I'm seik and
tired o listenin tae your sneerie tongue . . .

SANDY Hi, Wullie, what's this? Keep the heid, son, eh? Keep
the heid!

WAT (sneering) Cannae take it, eh?

WILL *pushes* SANDY *aside.*

WILL I tellt you tae shut up! Shut up — or you'll take it!
Ye'll take it frae me! Aaricht!

WAT Naw! No aaricht! I've taen about as muckle as I can
thole . . .

SANDY *tries to restrain* WAT.

93

SANDY   For the love o Christ, Wattie! Wad ye no . . .

WAT *throws* SANDY *to one side.*

WAT   Oot the road! Nae hauf-airsed wee pape's gonnae tell me . . .

WAT *draws his sword.* WILL *lets out a yell of anger and draws his sword too. He aims a great two-handed sweep in* WAT'S *direction. At that precise moment,* ANDREW *bursts in, hauling* WAT *out of the way of the blow and throwing him to one side.* WILL *is thrown off balance and the impetus of the blow spins him round.* ANDREW *grabs him by the belt and the scruff of the neck and throws him to the other side of the stage.*

ANDREW   What the fuckin hell dae you pair of stupit bastards think ye're airsin about at? I tellt ye, did I no? I tellt ye baith — but you, ye stupit fuckers, ye wadnae listen! *(Pauses breathless, exasperated with them.)* It's done! It's finished! And that's an end tae it!